Fremdsprachentexte

W. Somerset Maugham
The Letter

Herausgegeben von
Ulrich Hiller

Philipp Reclam jun. Stuttgart

Universal-Bibliothek Nr. 9183

Gesamtherstellung: Reclam, Ditzingen
Printed in Germany 1985
ISBN 3-15-009183-7

The Letter

Outside on the quay the sun beat fiercely. A stream of motors, lorries and buses, private cars and hirelings, sped up and down the crowded thoroughfare, and every chauffeur blew his horn; rickshaws threaded their nimble path amid the throng, and the panting coolies found breath to yell at one another; coolies, carrying heavy bales, sidled along with their quick jog-trot and shouted to the passer-by to make way; itinerant vendors proclaimed their wares. Singapore is the meeting-place of a hundred peoples; and men of all colours, black Tamils, yellow Chinks, brown Malays, Armenians, Jews and

2 **quay:** Kai; Uferstraße.
3 **hireling:** Mietwagen.
4 **to speed:** eilen, sausen.
thoroughfare: Durchgangsstraße.
5 **horn:** Hupe.
rickshaw: Rikscha.
nimble: flink, behend.
5f. **to thread one's path:** (fig.) sich durchschlängeln.
6 **throng:** Gedränge.
to pant: keuchen.
coolie: Kuli.
7 **to yell:** schreien.
8 **bale:** Last; Packen.
to sidle along: sich seitwärts fortbewegen.
jog-trot: Trab.
9 **itinerant vendor:** Straßenhändler.
9f. **to proclaim:** hier: anpreisen.
11 **Tamils:** Tamilen (indischer Volksstamm).
12 **Chinks** (slang, pej.): Chinesen.

Bengalis, called to one another in raucous tones. But inside the office of Messrs. Ripley, Joyce and Naylor it was pleasantly cool; it was dark after the dusty glitter of the street and agreeably quiet after its unceasing din. Mr. Joyce sat in his private room, at the table, with an electric fan turned full on him. He was leaning back, his elbows on the arms of the chair, with the tips of the outstretched fingers of one hand resting neatly against the tips of the outstretched fingers of the other. His gaze rested on the battered volumes of the Law Reports which stood on a long shelf in front of him. On the top of a cupboard were square boxes of japanned tin, on which were painted the names of various clients.

There was a knock at the door.

"Come in."

A Chinese clerk, very neat in his white ducks, opened it.

"Mr. Crosbie is here, sir."

He spoke beautiful English, accenting each word with precision, and Mr. Joyce had often wondered at the extent

1 **raucous:** rauh; heiser.
2 **Messrs.:** Abk. für *Messieurs* als Bezeichnung für Geschäftspartner.
3 **glitter:** Glanz; Flimmern.
4 **unceasing:** unaufhörlich.
din: Lärm, Getöse.
5f. **electric fan:** Ventilator.
8 **neatly** (adv.): ordentlich; präzis; schmuck.
9 **gaze:** (starrer) Blick.
10 **battered:** abgestoßen; ramponiert.
Law Reports: Urteilssammlungen.
12 **boxes of japanned tin:** lackierte Blechdosen.
13 **client:** Kunde; Klient.
16 **ducks** (pl.): Leinenhose.
18 **to accent:** betonen.
19 **extent:** Ausmaß; Umfang.

of his vocabulary. Ong Chi Seng was a Cantonese, and he had studied law at Gray's Inn. He was spending a year or two with Messrs. Ripley, Joyce and Naylor in order to prepare himself for practice on his own account. He was industrious, obliging, and of exemplary character.

"Show him in," said Mr. Joyce.

He rose to shake hands with his visitor and asked him to sit down. The light fell on him as he did so. The face of Mr. Joyce remained in shadow. He was by nature a silent man, and now he looked at Robert Crosbie for quite a minute without speaking. Crosbie was a big fellow, well over six feet high, with broad shoulders, and muscular. He was a rubber-planter, hard with the constant exercise of walking over the estate, and with the tennis which was his relaxation when the day's work was over. He was deeply sunburned. His hairy hands, his feet in clumsy boots were enormous, and Mr. Joyce found himself thinking that a blow of that great fist would easily kill the fragile Tamil. But there was no fierceness in his blue

1 **Cantonese:** Einwohner von Kanton (chinesische Großstadt).
2 **Gray's Inn:** Londoner Rechtsschule.
4 **on his own account:** für sich selbst.
5 **industrious:** arbeitsam, fleißig.
obliging: beflissen; zuvorkommend.
exemplary: beispielhaft.
7 **to show s.o. in:** jdn. hereinführen.
14 **rubber-planter:** Kautschukpflanzer.
14 f. **hard with the constant exercise of walking:** etwa: durch das ständige Gehen körperlich gestählt.
15 **estate:** Landgut; Anwesen.
16 **relaxation:** Entspannung.
17 **clumsy:** klobig, plump.
20 **fragile:** zerbrechlich, zart.
fierceness: Wildheit.

eyes; they were confiding and gentle; and his face, with its big, undistinguished features, was open, frank and honest. But at this moment it bore a look of deep distress. It was drawn and haggard.

"You look as though you hadn't had much sleep the last night or two," said Mr. Joyce.

"I haven't."

Mr. Joyce noticed now the old felt hat, with its broad double brim, which Crosbie had placed on the table; and then his eyes travelled to the khaki shorts he wore, showing his red hairy thighs, the tennis shirt open at the neck, without a tie, and the dirty khaki jacket with the ends of the sleeves turned up. He looked as though he had just come in from a long tramp among the rubber trees. Mr. Joyce gave a slight frown.

"You must pull yourself together, you know. You must keep your head."

"Oh, I'm all right."

"Have you seen your wife to-day?"

"No, I'm to see her this afternoon. You know, it is a damned shame that they should have arrested her."

"I think they had to do that," Mr. Joyce answered in his level, soft tone.

1 **confiding:** vertrauensvoll.
2 **undistinguished features:** wenig ausdrucksvolle Gesichtszüge.
3 **look:** hier: Ausdruck, Aussehen.
3f. **distress:** Kummer, Not.
4 **drawn:** hier: verzerrt, verzogen.
haggard: abgemagert; abgehärmt.
8 **felt:** Filz.
9 **brim:** Hutrand, Krempe.
11 **thigh:** Oberschenkel.
14 **tramp:** Fußmarsch.
15 **to give a slight frown:** leicht die Stirn runzeln.
23 **level:** gleichmäßig; ausgeglichen.

"I should have thought they'd have let her out on bail."
"It's a very serious charge."
"It is damnable. She did what any decent woman would do in her place. Only, nine women out of ten wouldn't have the pluck. Leslie's the best woman in the world. She wouldn't hurt a fly. Why, hang it all, man, I've been married to her for twelve years, do you think I don't know her? God, if I'd got hold of the man I'd have wrung his neck, I'd have killed him without a moment's hesitation. So would you."
"My dear fellow, everybody's on your side. No one has a good word to say for Hammond. We're going to get her off. I don't suppose either the assessors or the judge will go into court without having already made up their minds to bring in a verdict of not guilty."
"The whole thing's a farce," said Crosbie violently. "She ought never to have been arrested in the first place, and then it's terrible, after all the poor girl's gone through, to subject her to the ordeal of a trial. There's not a soul I've

1 **on bail:** gegen Kaution.
2 **charge:** Beschuldigung.
3 **damnable:** schändlich.
decent: anständig; sittsam.
5 **pluck:** Mut.
6 **hang it all:** zum Henker!
8 f. **to wring s.o.'s neck:** jdm. den Hals umdrehen.
9 f. **hesitation:** Zögern; Bedenken.
12 f. **to get s.o. off:** jdn. freibekommen, herausholen (aus dem Gefängnis).
13 **assessor:** Beisitzer.
15 **to bring in a verdict of not guilty:** für nicht schuldig befinden.
17 **in the first place:** überhaupt.
18 **to go through s.th.:** etwas durchmachen.
19 **to subject:** unterwerfen; unterziehen.
ordeal: (Nerven-)Probe.
trial: Verhör; Gerichtsverhandlung; Prozeß.

met since I've been in Singapore, man or woman, who hasn't told me that Leslie was absolutely justified. I think it's awful to keep her in prison all these weeks."

"The law is the law. After all, she confesses that she killed the man. It is terrible, and I'm dreadfully sorry for both you and for her."

"I don't matter a hang," interrupted Crosbie.

"But the fact remains that murder has been committed, and in a civilised community a trial is inevitable."

"Is it murder to exterminate noxious vermin? She shot him as she would have shot a mad dog."

Mr. Joyce leaned back again in his chair and once more placed the tips of his ten fingers together. The little construction he formed looked like the skeleton of a roof. He was silent for a moment.

"I should be wanting in my duty as your legal adviser," he said at last, in an even voice, looking at his client with his cool, brown eyes, "if I did not tell you that there is one point which causes me just a little anxiety. If your wife had only shot Hammond once, the whole thing would be absolutely plain sailing. Unfortunately she fired six times."

2 **to be absolutely justified:** völlig im Recht sein.
7 **I don't matter a hang:** das ist mir völlig schnuppe.
8 **to commit:** begehen (Verbrechen).
9 **inevitable:** unvermeidlich.
10 **to exterminate:** ausrotten.
noxious: schädlich.
vermin: Ungeziefer.
14 **skeleton:** Skelett; Gerüst.
16 **I should be wanting in my duty:** ich würde meine Pflicht verletzen.
legal adviser: Rechtsbeistand.
17 **even:** gelassen; gleichmütig.
21 **plain sailing:** hier etwa: eine einfache Geschichte.

"Her explanation is perfectly simple. In the circumstances anyone would have done the same."
"I dare say," said Mr. Joyce, "and of course I think the explanation is very reasonable. But it's no good closing our eyes to the facts. It's always a good plan to put yourself in another man's place, and I can't deny that if I were prosecuting for the Crown that is the point on which I should centre my enquiry."
"My dear fellow, that's perfectly idiotic."
Mr. Joyce shot a sharp glance at Robert Crosbie. The shadow of a smile hovered over his shapely lips. Crosbie was a good fellow, but he could hardly be described as intelligent.
"I dare say it's of no importance," answered the lawyer, "I just thought it was a point worth mentioning. You haven't got very long to wait now, and when it's all over I recommend you to go off somewhere with your wife on a trip, and forget all about it. Even though we are almost dead certain to get an acquittal, a trial of that sort is anxious work, and you'll both want a rest."
For the first time Crosbie smiled, and his smile strangely changed his face. You forgot the uncouthness and saw only the goodness of his soul.

3 **I dare say:** etwa: allerdings.
7 **to prosecute:** die Anklage vertreten; verfolgen.
8 **to centre:** konzentrieren.
enquiry: Untersuchung.
10 **to shoot a glance:** einen Blick werfen.
11 **to hover:** schweben.
shapely: wohlgeformt.
17 **to recommend:** empfehlen.
19 **acquittal:** Freispruch.
20 **anxious:** hier: nervenaufreibend.
22 **uncouthness:** Unbeholfenheit; Grobschlächtigkeit.

"I think I shall want it more than Leslie. She's borne up wonderfully. By God, there's a plucky little woman for you."

"Yes, I've been very much struck by her self-control," said the lawyer. "I should never have guessed that she was capable of such determination."

His duties as her counsel had made it necessary for him to have a good many interviews with Mrs. Crosbie since her arrest. Though things had been made as easy as could be for her, the fact remained that she was in gaol, awaiting her trial for murder, and it would not have been surprising if her nerves had failed her. She appeared to bear her ordeal with composure. She read a great deal, took such exercise as was possible, and by favour of the authorities worked at the pillow lace which had always formed the entertainment of her long hours of leisure. When Mr. Joyce saw her, she was neatly dressed in cool, fresh, simple frocks, her hair was carefully arranged, and her nails were manicured. Her manner was collected. She

1 **she's borne up:** sie hat sich wieder gefangen.
2 **plucky:** mutig; couragiert.
4 **to be struck by s.th.:** von etwas beeindruckt sein.
6 **determination:** Entschlossenheit.
7 **counsel:** Anwalt.
10 **gaol:** Gefängnis.
12 **to fail s.o.:** jdn. im Stich lassen.
13 **composure:** Fassung.
13f. **to take exercise:** sich Bewegung verschaffen.
14 **favour:** hier: Erlaubnis.
15 **pillow lace:** Klöppelspitze.
16 **leisure:** Muße.
18 **frock:** Kleid; Kittel.
19 **to manicure:** maniküren, (Hände) pflegen.
collected: gesammelt, gefaßt.

was able even to jest upon the little inconveniences of her position. There was something casual about the way in which she spoke of the tragedy, which suggested to Mr. Joyce that only her good breeding prevented her from finding something a trifle ludicrous in a situation which was eminently serious. It surprised him, for he had never thought that she had a sense of humour.

He had known her off and on for a good many years. When she paid visits to Singapore she generally came to dine with his wife and himself, and once or twice she had passed a week-end with them at their bungalow by the sea. His wife had spent a fortnight with her on the estate, and had met Geoffrey Hammond several times. The two couples had been on friendly, if not on intimate, terms, and it was on this account that Robert Crosbie had rushed over to Singapore immediately after the catastrophe and begged Mr. Joyce to take charge personally of his unhappy wife's defence.

The story she told him the first time he saw her she had never varied in the smallest detail. She told it as coolly then, a few hours after the tragedy, as she told it now.

1 **to jest:** scherzen.
inconvenience: Unannehmlichkeit.
2 **casual:** beiläufig; lässig.
3 **to suggest to s.o.:** hier: jdm. andeuten, nahelegen.
4 **breeding:** Erziehung.
5 **a trifle:** ein bißchen.
ludicrous: komisch; lächerlich.
8 **off and on:** mit Unterbrechungen.
14 **to be on friendly terms with s.o.:** mit jdm. auf freundschaftlichem Fuß stehen, befreundet sein.
15 **on this account:** aus diesem Grund.
17 f. **to take charge of s.o.'s defence:** jds. Verteidigung übernehmen.
20 **to vary:** abwandeln.

She told it connectedly, in a level, even voice, and her only sign of confusion was when a slight colour came into her cheeks as she described one or two of its incidents. She was the last woman to whom one would have expected such a thing to happen. She was in the early thirties, a fragile creature, neither short nor tall, and graceful rather than pretty. Her wrists and ankles were very delicate, but she was extremely thin, and you could see the bones of her hands through the white skin, and the veins were large and blue. Her face was colourless, slightly sallow, and her lips were pale. You did not notice the colour of her eyes. She had a great deal of light brown hair, and it had a slight natural wave; it was the sort of hair that with a little touching-up would have been very pretty, but you could not imagine that Mrs. Crosbie would think of resorting to any such device. She was a quiet, pleasant, unassuming woman. Her manner was engaging, and if she was not very popular it was because she suffered from a certain shyness. This was comprehensible enough, for the planter's life is lonely, and in her own house, with people she knew, she was in her

1 **connectedly** (adv.): zusammenhängend.
7 **graceful:** anmutig.
wrist: Handgelenk.
ankle: Knöchel; Fußgelenk.
8 **delicate:** zart.
11 **sallow:** fahl.
14 **touching-up:** Zurechtmachen.
16 **to resort to s.th.:** zu etwas greifen; Zuflucht nehmen zu.
device: Mittel; Kunstgriff.
17 **unassuming:** bescheiden.
17f. **her manner was engaging:** sie war von gewinnender Art.
19 **shyness:** Schüchternheit; Scheu.
19f. **comprehensible:** begreiflich.

quiet way charming. Mrs. Joyce, after her fortnight's stay, had told her husband that Leslie was a very agreeable hostess. There was more in her, she said, than people thought; and when you came to know her you were surprised how much she had read and how entertaining she could be.

She was the last woman in the world to commit murder.

Mr. Joyce dismissed Robert Crosbie with such reassuring words as he could find and, once more alone in his office, turned over the pages of the brief. But it was a mechanical action, for all its details were familiar to him. The case was the sensation of the day, and it was discussed in all the clubs, at all the dinner tables, up and down the Peninsula, from Singapore to Penang. The facts that Mrs. Crosbie gave were simple. Her husband had gone to Singapore on business, and she was alone for the night. She dined by herself, late, at a quarter to nine, and after dinner sat in the sitting-room working at her lace. It opened on the verandah. There was no one in the bungalow, for the servants had retired to their own quarters at the back of the compound. She was surprised to hear a step on the gravel path in the garden, a booted step, which suggested a white man rather than a native, for she had not heard a motor drive up, and she could not imagine who could be coming to see her at that time of

3 **hostess:** Gastgeberin.
8 **to dismiss:** verabschieden; entlassen.
reassuring: beruhigend.
10 **brief:** Schriftsatz.
13 f. **peninsula:** Halbinsel.
20 **quarters:** Unterkünfte.
21 **compound:** (Eingeborenen-)Siedlung, Dorf.
22 **gravel:** Kies.

night. Someone ascended the few stairs that led up to the bungalow, walked across the verandah, and appeared at the door of the room in which she sat. At the first moment she did not recognise the visitor. She sat with a shaded lamp, and he stood with his back to the darkness.

"May I come in?" he said.

She did not even recognise the voice.

"Who is it?" she asked.

She worked with spectacles, and she took them off as she spoke.

"Geoff. Hammond."

"Of course. Come in and have a drink."

She rose and shook hands with him cordially. She was a little surprised to see him, for though he was a neighbour neither she nor Robert had been lately on very intimate terms with him, and she had not seen him for some weeks. He was the manager of a rubber estate nearly eight miles from theirs, and she wondered why he had chosen this late hour to come and see them.

"Robert's away," she said. "He had to go to Singapore for the night."

Perhaps he thought his visit called for some explanation, for he said:

"I'm sorry. I felt rather lonely to-night, so I thought I'd just come along and see how you were getting on."

"How on earth did you come? I never heard a car."

1 **to ascend:** hochsteigen.
5 **shaded:** (mit einem Schirm) abgedunkelt.
14 **cordially** (adv.): herzlich.
16 **lately:** unlängst; seit kurzem.
23 **to call for s.th.:** etwas verlangen, erforderlich machen.

"I left it down the road. I thought you might both be in bed and asleep."

This was natural enough. The planter gets up at dawn in order to take the roll-call of the workers, and soon after dinner he is glad to go to bed. Hammond's car was in point of fact found next day a quarter of a mile from the bungalow.

Since Robert was away there was no whisky and soda in the room. Leslie did not call the boy, who was probably asleep, but fetched it herself. Her guest mixed himself a drink and filled his pipe.

Geoff. Hammond had a host of friends in the colony. He was at this time in the late thirties, but he had come out as a lad. He had been one of the first to volunteer on the outbreak of war, and had done very well. A wound in the knee caused him to be invalided out of the army after two years, but he returned to the Federated Malay States with a D. S. O. and an M. C. He was one of the best billiard-players in the colony. He had been a beautiful dancer and a fine tennis-player, but though able no longer to dance, and his tennis, with a stiff knee, was not so good as it had been, he had the gift of popularity and was universally liked. He was a tall, good-looking fellow,

4 **roll-call:** Anwesenheitskontrolle.
5 f. **in point of fact:** in der Tat.
12 **host:** Menge.
13 **to come out:** hier: in die Kolonien kommen.
14 **lad:** junger Bursche.
to volunteer: sich freiwillig melden.
16 **to invalid:** dienstuntauglich machen.
17 **Federated Malay States:** Malaiischer Bundesstaat.
18 **D. S. O.:** Abk. für *Distinguished Service Order* (hohe militärische Auszeichnung).
M. C.: Abk. für *Military Cross* (hohe militärische Auszeichnung).

with attractive blue eyes and a fine head of black, curling hair. Old stagers said his only fault was that he was too fond of the girls, and after the catastrophe they shook their heads and vowed that they had always known this would get him into trouble.

He began now to talk to Leslie about the local affairs, the forthcoming races in Singapore, the price of rubber, and his chances of killing a tiger which had been lately seen in the neighbourhood. She was anxious to finish by a certain date the piece of lace on which she was working, for she wanted to send it home for her mother's birthday, and so put on her spectacles again, and drew towards her chair the little table on which stood the pillow.

"I wish you wouldn't wear those great horn-spectacles," he said. "I don't know why a pretty woman should do her best to look plain."

She was a trifle taken aback at this remark. He had never used that tone with her before. She thought the best thing was to make light of it.

"I have no pretensions to being a raving beauty, you know, and if you ask me point-blank, I'm bound to tell

1 **to curl:** (sich) kräuseln.
2 **old stagers:** (fig.) alte Hasen.
4 **to vow:** versichern; feierlich erklären.
7 **forthcoming:** bevorstehend.
14 **pillow:** hier: Klöppelkissen.
17 **plain:** unansehnlich; häßlich.
18 **to be taken aback:** verblüfft sein.
20 **to make light of s.th.:** über etwas hinweggehen.
21 **pretension:** Anspruch.
raving: hinreißend, rasend.
22 **point-blank:** rundheraus.
to be bound to do s.th.: etwas (zwangsläufig) tun müssen.

you that I don't care two pins if you think me plain or not."

"I don't think you're plain. I think you're awfully pretty."

"Sweet of you," she answered, ironically. "But in that case I can only think you half-witted."

He chuckled. But he rose from his chair and sat down in another by her side.

"You're not going to have the face to deny that you have the prettiest hands in the world," he said.

He made a gesture as though to take one of them. She gave him a little tap.

"Don't be an idiot. Sit down where you were before and talk sensibly, or else I shall send you home."

He did not move.

"Don't you know that I'm awfully in love with you?" he said.

She remained quite cool.

"I don't. I don't believe it for a minute, and even if it were true I don't want you to say it."

She was the more surprised at what he was saying, since during the seven years she had known him he had never paid her any particular attention. When he came back from the war they had seen a good deal of one another, and once when he was ill Robert had gone over and brought him back to their bungalow in his car. He had stayed with them for a fortnight. But their interests were

1 **I don't care two pins:** es kümmert mich nicht im geringsten.
6 **half-witted:** nicht recht bei Trost.
7 **to chuckle:** kichern.
9 **to have the face to do s.th.:** die Kühnheit haben, etwas zu tun.
12 **tap:** Klaps.
14 **sensibly** (adv.): vernünftig.

dissimilar, and the acquaintance had never ripened into friendship. For the last two or three years they had seen little of him. Now and then he came over to play tennis, now and then they met him at some planter's who was giving a party, but it often happened that they did not set eyes on him for a month at a time.

Now he took another whisky and soda. Leslie wondered if he had been drinking before. There was something odd about him, and it made her a trifle uneasy. She watched him help himself with disapproval.

"I wouldn't drink any more if I were you," she said, good-humouredly still.

He emptied his glass and put it down.

"Do you think I'm talking to you like this because I'm drunk?" he asked abruptly.

"That is the most obvious explanation, isn't it?"

"Well, it's a lie. I've loved you ever since I first knew you. I've held my tongue as long as I could, and now it's got to come out. I love you, I love you, I love you."

She rose and carefully put aside the pillow.

"Good-night," she said.

"I'm not going now."

At last she began to lose her temper.

"But, you poor fool, don't you know that I've never

1 **dissimilar:** ungleich; verschieden.
acquaintance: Bekanntschaft; Bekannte(r).
to ripen: reifen.
6 **for a month at a time:** einen ganzen Monat lang.
8 **odd:** eigentümlich.
9 **uneasy:** unbehaglich.
10 **disapproval:** Mißbilligung.
12 **good-humouredly** (adv.): gut gelaunt; gutmütig.
16 **obvious:** offenkundig.
23 **to lose one's temper:** die Beherrschung verlieren.

loved anyone but Robert, and even if I didn't love Robert you're the last man I should care for."
"What do I care? Robert's away."
"If you don't go away this minute I shall call the boys, and have you thrown out."
"They're out of earshot."
She was very angry now. She made a movement as though to go on to the verandah, from which the house-boy would certainly hear her, but he seized her arm.
"Let me go," she cried furiously.
"Not much. I've got you now."
She opened her mouth and called "Boy, boy," but with a quick gesture he put his hand over it. Then before she knew what he was about he had taken her in his arms and was kissing her passionately. She struggled, turning her lips away from his burning mouth.
"No, no, no," she cried. "Leave me alone. I won't."
She grew confused about what happened then. All that had been said before she remembered accurately, but now his words assailed her ears through a mist of horror and fear. He seemed to plead for her love. He broke into violent protestations of passion. And all the time he held her in his tempestuous embrace. She was helpless, for he was a strong, powerful man, and her arms were pinioned to her sides; her struggles were unavailing, and she felt

6 **out of earshot:** außer Hörweite.
15 **passionately** (adv.): leidenschaftlich.
20 **to assail:** bestürmen.
21 **to plead:** flehen.
22 **protestation:** Beteuerung.
23 **tempestuous:** stürmisch.
embrace: Umarmung.
24 **to pinion:** fesseln.
25 **unavailing:** nutzlos.

herself grow weaker; she was afraid she would faint, and his hot breath on her face made her feel desperately sick. He kissed her mouth, her eyes, her cheeks, her hair. The pressure of his arms was killing her. He lifted her off her feet. She tried to kick him, but he only held her more closely. He was carrying her now. He wasn't speaking any more, but she knew that his face was pale and his eyes hot with desire. He was taking her into the bedroom. He was no longer a civilised man, but a savage. And as he ran he stumbled against a table which was in the way. His stiff knee made him a little awkward on his feet, and with the burden of the woman in his arms he fell. In a moment she had snatched herself away from him. She ran round the sofa. He was up in a flash, and flung himself towards her. There was a revolver on the desk. She was not a nervous woman, but Robert was to be away for the night, and she had meant to take it into her room when she went to bed. That was why it happened to be there. She was frantic with terror now. She did not know what she was doing. She heard a report. She saw Hammond stagger. He gave a cry. He said something, she didn't know what. He lurched out of the room on to the verandah. She was in a frenzy now, she was

1 **to faint:** in Ohnmacht fallen.
9 **savage:** Wilder.
11 **awkward:** ungeschickt; unbeholfen.
13 **to snatch o.s. away:** sich losreißen.
14 **in a flash:** im Nu.
15 **to fling o.s.:** sich stürzen.
19 **frantic:** von Sinnen; rasend.
20 **report:** Schuß, Knall.
21 **to stagger:** straucheln; taumeln.
22 **to lurch:** torkeln.
23 **frenzy:** Raserei.

 stoßen (stolpern)

beside herself, she followed him out, yes, that was it, she must have followed him out, though she remembered nothing of it, she followed firing automatically, shot after shot, till the six chambers were empty. Hammond fell down on the floor of the verandah. He crumpled up into a bloody heap.

When the boys, startled by the reports, rushed up, they found her standing over Hammond with the revolver still in her hand and Hammond lifeless. She looked at them for a moment without speaking. They stood in a frightened, huddled bunch. She let the revolver fall from her hand, and without a word turned and went into the sitting-room. They watched her go into her bedroom and turn the key in the lock. They dared not touch the dead body, but looked at it with terrified eyes, talking excitedly to one another in undertones. Then the head-boy collected himself; he had been with them for many years, he was Chinese and a level-headed fellow. Robert had gone into Singapore on his motor-cycle, and the car stood in the garage. He told the seis to get it out; they must go at once to the Assistant District Officer and tell him what had happened. He picked up the revolver and

4 **chamber:** (Revolver-)Kammer.
5 **to crumple up:** zusammensacken; zusammenbrechen.
7 **startled:** aufgeschreckt.
to rush up: herbeieilen.
11 **huddled:** zusammengedrängt.
bunch: Bündel; Haufen; Gruppe.
15 f. **to talk in undertones:** flüstern.
17 **to collect o.s.:** sich fassen.
18 **level-headed:** ausgeglichen; besonnen.
20 **seis:** Garagenbursche.
21 **Assistant District Officer:** etwa: stellvertretender Bezirksverwalter (Abk.: *A. D. O.*).

put it in his pocket. The A. D. O., a man called Withers, lived on the outskirts of the nearest town, which was about thirty-five miles away. It took them an hour and a half to reach him. Everyone was asleep, and they had to rouse the boys. Presently Withers came out and they told him their errand. The head-boy showed him the revolver in proof of what he said. The A. D. O. went into his room to dress, sent for his car, and in a little while was following them back along the deserted road. The dawn was just breaking as he reached the Crosbies' bungalow. He ran up the steps of the verandah, and stopped short as he saw Hammond's body lying where he fell. He touched the face. It was quite cold.

"Where's mem?" he asked the house-boy.

The Chinese pointed to the bedroom. Withers went to the door and knocked. There was no answer. He knocked again.

"Mrs. Crosbie," he called.

"Who is it?"

"Withers."

There was another pause. Then the door was unlocked and slowly opened. Leslie stood before him. She had not been to bed, and wore the tea-gown in which she had dined. She stood and looked silently at the A. D. O.

"Your house-boy fetched me," he said. "Hammond. What have you done?"

"He tried to rape me, and I shot him."

2 **outskirts** (pl.): Außenbezirk; Vorort.
6 **errand:** Auftrag.
14 **mem:** Hausherrin.
23 **tea-gown:** Nachmittagskleid.
27 **to rape:** vergewaltigen.

"My God. I say, you'd better come out here. You must tell me exactly what happened."

"Not now. I can't. You must give me time. Send for my husband."

Withers was a young man, and he did not know exactly what to do in an emergency which was so out of the run of his duties. Leslie refused to say anything till at last Robert arrived. Then she told the two men the story, from which since then, though she had repeated it over and over again, she had never in the slightest degree diverged.

The point to which Mr. Joyce recurred was the shooting. As a lawyer he was bothered that Leslie had fired not once, but six times, and the examination of the dead man showed that four of the shots had been fired close to the body. One might almost have thought that when the man fell she stood over him and emptied the contents of the revolver into him. She confessed that her memory, so accurate for all that had preceded, failed her here. Her mind was blank. It pointed to an uncontrollable fury; but uncontrollable fury was the last thing you would have expected from this quiet and demure woman. Mr. Joyce had known her a good many years, and had always thought her an unemotional person; during the weeks

6 **emergency:** Notfall.
run: (fig.) Verlauf, Gang.
11 **to diverge:** abweichen.
12 **to recur:** zurückkommen.
13 **to bother:** beunruhigen.
19 **to precede:** vorausgehen.
20 **blank:** leer.
fury: Raserei; Wut.
22 **demure:** nüchtern; besonnen.

that had passed since the tragedy her composure had been amazing.

Mr. Joyce shrugged his shoulders.

"The fact is, I suppose," he reflected, "that you can never tell what hidden possibilities of savagery there are in the most respectable of women."

There was a knock at the door.

"Come in."

The Chinese clerk entered and closed the door behind him. He closed it gently, with deliberation, but decidedly, and advanced to the table at which Mr. Joyce was sitting.

"May I trouble you, sir, for a few words private conversation?" he said.

The elaborate accuracy with which the clerk expressed himself always faintly amused Mr. Joyce, and now he smiled.

"It's no trouble, Chi Seng," he replied.

"The matter on which I desire to speak to you, sir, is delicate and confidential."

"Fire away."

Mr. Joyce met his clerk's shrewd eyes. As usual Ong Chi Seng was dressed in the height of local fashion. He wore

3 **to shrug:** (die Schultern) zucken.
5 **savagery:** Wildheit; Barbarei.
6 **respectable:** achtbar; anständig.
10 **deliberation:** Überlegung; Behutsamkeit.
10f. **decidedly** (adv.): entschieden; bestimmt.
15 **elaborate:** gewählt; durchdacht; vollendet.
accuracy: Genauigkeit.
20 **delicate:** hier: heikel.
confidential: vertraulich.
21 **to fire away** (coll.): losschießen, loslegen, anfangen.
22 **shrewd:** schlau; scharfsinnig.
23 **in the height of fashion:** nach der neuesten Mode.

very shiny patent-leather shoes and gay silk socks. In his black tie was a pearl and ruby pin, and on the fourth finger of his left hand a diamond ring. From the pocket of his neat white coat protruded a gold fountain pen and a gold pencil. He wore a gold wrist-watch, and on the bridge of his nose invisible pince-nez. He gave a little cough.

"The matter has to do with the case R. *v.* Crosbie, sir."

"Yes?"

"A circumstance has come to my knowledge, sir, which seems to me to put a different complexion on it."

"What circumstance?"

"It has come to my knowledge, sir, that there is a letter in existence from the defendant to the unfortunate victim of the tragedy."

"I shouldn't be at all surprised. In the course of the last seven years I have no doubt that Mrs. Crosbie often had occasion to write to Mr. Hammond."

Mr. Joyce had a high opinion of his clerk's intelligence and his words were designed to conceal his thoughts.

"That is very probable, sir. Mrs. Crosbie must have communicated with the deceased frequently, to invite him to dine with her for example, or to propose a tennis game. That was my first thought when the matter was brought

1 **patent-leather:** Lackleder.
gay: bunt.
2 **ruby:** Rubin.
4 **to protrude:** herausragen.
5 **bridge:** (Nasen-)Rücken.
6 **pince-nez** (frz.): Kneifer.
7 **R. *v.* Crosbie:** Abk. für *Rex versus Crosbie* ›der König gegen Crosbie‹.
10 **complexion:** (fig.) Aussehen.
13 **defendant:** Angeklagte(r).
19 **to design:** bestimmen.
to conceal: verbergen.
21 **the deceased:** der Verstorbene.

Perle 2 Füllfederhalter

to my notice. This letter, however, was written on the day of the late Mr. Hammond's death."

Mr. Joyce did not flicker an eyelash. He continued to look at Ong Chi Seng with the smile of faint amusement with which he generally talked to him.

"Who has told you this?"

"The circumstances were brought to my knowledge, sir, by a friend of mine."

Mr. Joyce knew better than to insist.

"You will no doubt recall, sir, that Mrs. Crosbie has stated that until the fatal night she had had no communication with the deceased for several weeks."

"Have you got the letter?"

"No, sir."

"What are its contents?"

"My friend gave me a copy. Would you like to peruse it, sir?"

"I should."

Ong Chi Seng took from an inside pocket a bulky wallet. It was filled with papers, Singapore dollar notes and cigarette cards. From the confusion he presently extracted a half-sheet of thin notepaper and placed it before Mr. Joyce. The letter read as follows: —

1 **notice:** hier: Beachtung; Kenntnis.
2 **late:** hier: verstorben; selig.
3 **to flicker:** zucken.
eyelash: Wimper.
10 **to recall:** sich entsinnen.
11 **fatal:** unheilvoll; verhängnisvoll.
16 **to peruse:** (durch)lesen; prüfen.
19 **bulky:** sperrig; vollgestopft.
wallet: Brieftasche.
21 **confusion:** hier: Durcheinander, Wirrwarr.
22 **to extract:** herausziehen.
23 **The letter read as follows:** Der Brief lautete wie folgt.

R. will be away for the night. I absolutely must see you. I shall expect you at eleven. I am desperate, and if you don't come I won't answer for the consequences. Don't drive up. — L.

It was written in the flowing hand which the Chinese were taught at the foreign schools. The writing, so lacking in character, was oddly incongruous with the ominous words.

"What makes you think that this note was written by Mrs. Crosbie?"

"I have every confidence in the veracity of my informant, sir," replied Ong Chi Seng. "And the matter can very easily be put to the proof. Mrs. Crosbie will, no doubt, be able to tell you at once whether she wrote such a letter or not."

Since the beginning of the conversation Mr. Joyce had not taken his eyes off the respectable countenance of his clerk. He wondered now if he discerned in it a faint expression of mockery.

"It is inconceivable that Mrs. Crosbie should have written such a letter," said Mr. Joyce.

3 **to answer for the consequences:** für die Folgen einstehen.
5 **flowing:** fließend; flüssig.
hand: (Hand-)Schrift.
6f. **lacking in character:** nicht ausgeprägt; charakterlos.
7 **incongruous:** unvereinbar; im Widerstreit.
7f. **ominous:** unheilvoll.
11 **veracity:** Glaubwürdigkeit.
13 **to put to the proof:** überprüfen.
17 **countenance:** Gesichtsausdruck.
18 **to discern:** entdecken; erkennen.
19 **mockery:** Spott.
20 **inconceivable:** undenkbar; unvorstellbar.

"If that is your opinion, sir, the matter is of course ended. My friend spoke to me on the subject only because he thought, as I was in your office, you might like to know of the existence of this letter before a communication was made to the Deputy Public Prosecutor."

"Who has the original?" asked Mr. Joyce sharply.

Ong Chi Seng made no sign that he perceived in this question and its manner a change of attitude.

"You will remember, sir, no doubt, that after the death of Mr. Hammond it was discovered that he had had relations with a Chinese woman. The letter is at present in her possession."

That was one of the things which had turned public opinion most vehemently against Hammond. It came to be known that for several months he had had a Chinese woman living in his house.

For a moment neither of them spoke. Indeed everything had been said and each understood the other perfectly.

"I'm obliged to you, Chi Seng. I will give the matter my consideration."

"Very good, sir. Do you wish me to make a communication to that effect to my friend?"

"I dare say it would be as well if you kept in touch with him," Mr. Joyce answered with gravity.

"Yes, sir."

The clerk noiselessly left the room, shutting the door again with deliberation, and left Mr. Joyce to his reflec-

5 **Deputy Public Prosecutor:** stellvertretender Staatsanwalt.
14 **vehemently** (adv.): heftig.
19 **obliged:** verbunden, verpflichtet.
20 **consideration:** Überlegung.
22 **to that effect:** in diesem Sinn.
24 **gravity:** Ernst; Gemessenheit.

tions. He stared at the copy, in its neat, impersonal writing, of Leslie's letter. Vague suspicions troubled him. They were so disconcerting that he made an effort to put them out of his mind. There must be a simple explanation of the letter, and Leslie without doubt could give it at once, but, by heaven, an explanation was needed. He rose from his chair, put the letter in his pocket, and took his topee. When he went out Ong Chi Seng was busily writing at his desk.

"I'm going out for a few minutes, Chi Seng," he said.

"Mr. George Reed is coming by appointment at twelve o'clock, sir. Where shall I say you've gone?"

Mr. Joyce gave him a thin smile.

"You can say that you haven't the least idea."

But he knew perfectly well that Ong Chi Seng was aware that he was going to the gaol. Though the crime had been committed in Belanda and the trial was to take place at Belanda Bharu, since there was in the gaol no convenience for the detention of a white woman Mrs. Crosbie had been brought to Singapore.

When she was led into the room in which he waited she held out her thin, distinguished hand, and gave him a pleasant smile. She was as ever neatly and simply dressed, and her abundant, pale hair was arranged with care.

3 **to disconcert:** beunruhigen; aus der Fassung bringen.
8 **topee:** Tropenhelm.
11 **by appointment:** wie verabredet.
18 f. **convenience:** Einrichtung.
19 **detention:** Haft.
22 **distinguished:** vornehm.
24 **abundant:** üppig.

"I wasn't expecting to see you this morning," she said, graciously.
She might have been in her own house, and Mr. Joyce almost expected to hear her call the boy and tell him to bring the visitor a gin pahit.
"How are you?" he asked.
"I'm in the best of health, thank you." A flicker of amusement flashed across her eyes. "This is a wonderful place for a rest cure."
The attendant withdrew and they were left alone.
"Do sit down," said Leslie.
He took a chair. He did not quite know how to begin. She was so cool that it seemed almost impossible to say to her the thing he had come to say. Though she was not pretty there was something agreeable in her appearance. She had elegance, but it was the elegance of good breeding in which there was nothing of the artifice of society. You had only to look at her to know what sort of people she had and what kind of surroundings she had lived in. Her fragility gave her a singular refinement. It was impossible to associate her with the vaguest idea of grossness.

2 **graciously** (adv.): wohlwollend; freundlich.
5 **gin pahit:** bitterer Gin.
7 **flicker:** Flackern; Zucken.
8 **to flash:** aufblitzen.
9 **rest cure:** Erholungskur.
10 **attendant:** Wärter(in).
to withdraw: sich zurückziehen.
17 **artifice:** Raffinesse; Berechnung.
20 **fragility:** Zerbrechlichkeit.
singular: einzigartig.
refinement: Eleganz; Feinheit.
21 **to associate:** in Verbindung bringen.
grossness: Grobheit.

"I'm looking forward to seeing Robert this afternoon," she said, in her good-humoured, easy voice. (It was a pleasure to hear her speak, her voice and her accent were so distinctive of her class.) "Poor dear, it's been a great trial to his nerves. I'm thankful it'll all be over in a few days."

"It's only five days now."

"I know. Each morning when I awake I say to myself, 'one less.'" She smiled then. "Just as I used to do at school and the holidays were coming."

"By the way, am I right in thinking that you had no communication whatever with Hammond for several weeks before the catastrophe?"

"I'm quite positive of that. The last time we met was at a tennis-party at the MacFarrens. I don't think I said more than two words to him. They have two courts, you know, and we didn't happen to be in the same sets."

"And you haven't written to him?"

"Oh, no."

"Are you quite sure of that?"

"Oh, quite," she answered, with a little smile. "There was nothing I should write to him for except to ask him to dine or to play tennis, and I hadn't done either for months."

"At one time you'd been on fairly intimate terms with him. How did it happen that you had stopped asking him to anything?"

4 **distinctive:** kennzeichnend.
5 **trial:** hier: Zerreißprobe.
14 **positive:** hier: überzeugt.
16 **court:** Tennisplatz.
17 **set:** Satz (Tennis).
25 **at one time:** einst; früher einmal.

Mrs. Crosbie shrugged her thin shoulders.

"One gets tired of people. We hadn't anything very much in common. Of course, when he was ill Robert and I did everything we could for him, but the last year or two he'd been quite well, and he was very popular. He had a good many calls on his time, and there didn't seem to be any need to shower invitations upon him."

"Are you quite certain that was all?"

Mrs. Crosbie hesitated for a moment.

"Well, I may just as well tell you. It had come to our ears that he was living with a Chinese woman, and Robert said he wouldn't have him in the house, I had seen her myself."

Mr. Joyce was sitting in a straight-backed arm-chair, resting his chin on his hand, and his eyes were fixed on Leslie. Was it his fancy that, as she made this remark, her black pupils were filled on a sudden, for the fraction of a second, with a dull red light? The effect was startling. Mr. Joyce shifted in his chair. He placed the tips of his ten fingers together. He spoke very slowly, choosing his words.

"I think I should tell you that there is in existence a letter in your handwriting to Geoff. Hammond."

He watched her closely. She made no movement, nor did her face change colour, but she took a noticeable time to reply.

5f. **he had a good many calls on his time:** etwa: seine Zeit war ziemlich in Anspruch genommen.
7 **to shower:** niederprasseln lassen; häufen.
14 **straight-backed:** mit gerader Rückenlehne.
16 **fancy:** Einbildung.
17 **pupil:** Pupille.
fraction: Bruchteil.
19 **to shift:** rücken.

"In the past I've often sent him little notes to ask him to something or other, or to get me something when I knew he was going to Singapore."

"This letter asks him to come and see you because Robert was going to Singapore."

"That's impossible. I never did anything of the kind."

"You'd better read it for yourself."

He took it out of his pocket and handed it to her. She gave it a glance and with a smile of scorn handed it back to him.

"That's not my handwriting."

"I know, it's said to be an exact copy of the original."

She read the words now, and as she read a horrible change came over her. Her colourless face grew dreadful to look at. It turned green. The flesh seemed on a sudden to fall away and her skin was tightly stretched over the bones. Her lips receded, showing her teeth, so that she had the appearance of making a grimace.She stared at Mr. Joyce with eyes that started from their sockets. He was looking now at a gibbering death's head.

"What does it mean?" she whispered.

Her mouth was so dry that she could utter no more than a hoarse sound. It was no longer a human voice.

"That is for you to say," he answered.

"I didn't write it. I swear I didn't write it."

"Be very careful what you say. If the original is in your handwriting it would be useless to deny it."

9 **scorn:** Verachtung.
16 **tightly stretched:** straff gespannt.
17 **to recede:** zurückweichen.
19 **to start:** hier: heraustreten.
socket: Augenhöhle.
20 **to gibber:** wirr daherreden.
23 **hoarse:** heiser.

"It would be a forgery."
"It would be difficult to prove that. It would be easy to prove that it was genuine."
A shiver passed through her lean body. But great beads of sweat stood on her forehead. She took a handkerchief from her bag and wiped the palms of her hands. She glanced at the letter again and gave Mr. Joyce a sidelong look.
"It's not dated. If I had written it and forgotten all about it, it might have been written years ago. If you'll give me time, I'll try and remember the circumstances."
"I noticed there was no date. If this letter were in the hands of the prosecution they would cross-examine the boys. They would soon find out whether someone took a letter to Hammond on the day of his death."
Mrs. Crosbie clasped her hands violently and swayed in her chair so that he thought she would faint.
"I swear to you that I didn't write that letter."
Mr. Joyce was silent for a little while. He took his eyes from her distraught face, and looked down on the floor. He was reflecting.
"In these circumstances we need not go into the matter

1 **forgery:** Fälschung.
3 **genuine:** echt.
4 **shiver:** Schauder.
lean: mager.
4 f. **beads of sweat:** Schweißperlen.
6 **palm:** Handfläche.
7 **sidelong:** seitwärts, von der Seite.
13 **prosecution:** Anklage; Anklagevertreter.
to cross-examine: einem Kreuzverhör unterziehen.
16 **to clasp one's hands:** die Hände zusammenpressen.
to sway: schwanken.
20 **distraught:** verwirrt; verzerrt.

further," he said slowly, at last breaking the silence. "If the possessor of this letter sees fit to place it in the hands of the prosecution you will be prepared."

His words suggested that he had nothing more to say to her, but he made no movement of departure. He waited. To himself he seemed to wait a very long time. He did not look at Leslie, but he was conscious that she sat very still. She made no sound. At last it was he who spoke.

"If you have nothing more to say to me I think I'll be getting back to my office."

"What would anyone who read the letter be inclined to think that it meant?" she asked then.

"He'd know that you had told a deliberate lie," answered Mr. Joyce sharply.

"When?"

"You have stated definitely that you had had no communication with Hammond for at least three months."

"The whole thing has been a terrible shock to me. The events of that dreadful night have been a nightmare. It's not very strange if one detail has escaped my memory."

"It would be unfortunate, when your memory has reproduced so exactly every particular of your interview with Hammond, that you should have forgotten so important a point as that he came to see you in the bungalow on the night of his death at your express desire."

2 **to see fit:** für gut halten.
5 **departure:** Aufbruch; Abschied.
11 **to be inclined to do s.th.:** zu etwas neigen.
13 **deliberate:** vorsätzlich; überlegt; absichtlich.
16 **definitely** (adv.): mit Bestimmtheit.
19 **nightmare:** Alptraum.
23 **particular:** Einzelheit.
26 **express desire:** ausdrücklicher Wunsch.

"I hadn't forgotten. After what happened I was afraid to mention it. I thought you'd none of you believe my story if I admitted that he'd come at my invitation. I dare say it was stupid of me; but I lost my head, and after I'd said once that I'd had no communication with Hammond I was obliged to stick to it."

By now Leslie had recovered her admirable composure, and she met Mr. Joyce's appraising glance with candour. Her gentleness was very disarming.

"You will be required to explain, then, *why* you asked Hammond to come and see you when Robert was away for the night."

She turned her eyes full on the lawyer. He had been mistaken in thinking them insignificant, they were rather fine eyes, and unless he was mistaken they were bright now with tears. Her voice had a little break in it.

"It was a surprise I was preparing for Robert. His birthday is next month. I knew he wanted a new gun and you know I'm dreadfully stupid about sporting things. I wanted to talk to Geoff. about it. I thought I'd get him to order it for me."

"Perhaps the terms of the letter are not very clear to your recollection. Will you have another look at it?"

6 **to stick to s.th.:** bei etwas bleiben; an etwas festhalten.
7 **to recover:** wiedergewinnen, wiedererlangen.
8 **appraising:** prüfend; abschätzend; taxierend.
candour: Offenheit.
9 **gentleness:** Sanftmut.
disarming: entwaffnend.
13 f. **to be mistaken:** sich irren.
14 **insignificant:** bedeutungslos, unbedeutend.
16 **break:** hier: Umschlagen (der Stimme).
22 **terms** (pl.): hier: Wortlaut.
23 **recollection:** Erinnerung, Gedächtnis.

"No, I don't want to," she said quickly.

"Does it seem to you the sort of letter a woman would write to a somewhat distant acquaintance because she wanted to consult him about buying a gun?"

"I dare say it's rather extravagant and emotional. I do express myself like that, you know. I'm quite prepared to admit it's very silly." She smiled. "And after all, Geoff. Hammond wasn't quite a distant acquaintance. When he was ill I'd nursed him like a mother. I asked him to come when Robert was away, because Robert wouldn't have him in the house."

Mr. Joyce was tired of sitting so long in the same position. He rose and walked once or twice up and down the room, choosing the words he proposed to say; then he leaned over the back of the chair in which he had been sitting. He spoke slowly in a tone of deep gravity.

"Mrs. Crosbie, I want to talk to you very, very seriously. This case was comparatively plain sailing. There was only one point which seemed to me to require explanation: as far as I could judge, you had fired no less than four shots into Hammond when he was lying on the ground. It was hard to accept the possibility that a delicate, frightened, and habitually self-controlled woman, of gentle nature and refined instincts, should have surrendered to an absolutely uncontrolled frenzy. But of course it was admissible. Although Geoffrey Hammond was much liked and on the whole thought highly of, I was prepared to prove that he was the sort of man who might be guilty

23 **habitually** (adv.): normalerweise; gewöhnlich.
24 **refined:** verfeinert; fein.
to surrender: sich hinreißen lassen; sich ergeben.
26 **admissible:** zulässig.

of the crime which in justification of your act you accused him of. The fact, which was discovered after his death, that he had been living with a Chinese woman gave us something very definite to go upon. That robbed him of any sympathy which might have been felt for him. We made up our minds to make use of the odium which such a connection cast upon him in the minds of all respectable people. I told your husband this morning that I was certain of an acquittal, and I wasn't just telling him that to give him heart. I do not believe the assessors would have left the court."

They looked into one another's eyes. Mrs. Crosbie was strangely still. She was like a little bird paralysed by the fascination of a snake. He went on in the same quiet tones.

"But this letter has thrown an entirely different complexion on the case. I am your legal adviser, I shall represent you in court. I take your story as you tell it me, and I shall conduct your defence according to its terms. It may be that I believe your statements, and it may be that I doubt them. The duty of counsel is to persuade the court that the evidence placed before it is not such as to justify it in bringing in a verdict of guilty, and any private opinion he may have of the guilt or innocence of his client is entirely beside the point."

4 **to go upon s.th.:** hier: sich auf etwas stützen.
6 **odium:** Schimpf, Schande.
10 **to give s.o. heart:** jdm. Mut machen.
13 **to paralyse:** lähmen.
19 **to conduct:** führen.
terms: hier: (Geschäfts-)Bedingungen.
21 **to persuade:** überzeugen.
22 **evidence:** Beweis.
25 **beside the point:** unerheblich.

He was astonished to see in Leslie's eyes the flicker of a smile. Piqued, he went on somewhat dryly:
"You're not going to deny that Hammond came to your house at your urgent, and I may even say, hysterical invitation?"
Mrs. Crosbie, hesitating for an instant, seemed to consider.
"They can prove that the letter was taken to his bungalow by one of the house-boys. He rode over on his bicycle."
"You mustn't expect other people to be stupider than you. The letter will put them on the track of suspicions which have entered nobody's head. I will not tell you what I personally thought when I saw the copy. I do not wish you to tell me anything but what is needed to save your neck."
Mrs. Crosbie gave a shrill cry. She sprang to her feet, white with terror.
"You don't think they'd hang me?"
"If they came to the conclusion that you hadn't killed Hammond in self-defence, it would be the duty of the assessors to bring in a verdict of guilty. The charge is murder. It would be the duty of the judge to sentence you to death."
"But what can they prove?" she gasped.
"I don't know what they can prove. You know. I don't want to know. But if their suspicions are aroused, if they begin to make inquiries, if the natives are questioned – what is it that can be discovered?"

2 **piqued:** verärgert.
4 **urgent:** dringend, dringlich.
6f. **to consider:** hier: überlegen.
22 **to sentence:** verurteilen.
24 **to gasp:** keuchen.

She crumpled up suddenly. She fell on the floor before he could catch her. She had fainted. He looked round the room for water, but there was none there, and he did not want to be disturbed. He stretched her out on the floor, and kneeling beside her waited for her to recover. When she opened her eyes he was disconcerted by the ghastly fear that he saw in them.

"Keep quite still," he said. "You'll be better in a moment."

"You won't let them hang me," she whispered.

She began to cry, hysterically, while in undertones he sought to quieten her.

"For goodness sake pull yourself together," he said.

"Give me a minute."

Her courage was amazing. He could see the effort she made to regain her self-control, and soon she was once more calm.

"Let me get up now."

He gave her his hand and helped her to her feet. Taking her arm, he led her to the chair. She sat down wearily.

"Don't talk to me for a minute or two," she said.

"Very well."

When at last she spoke it was to say something which he did not expect. She gave a little sigh.

"I'm afraid I've made rather a mess of things," she said.

He did not answer, and once more there was a silence.

"Isn't it possible to get hold of the letter?" she said at last.

5 **to recover:** hier: sich erholen.
6 **ghastly:** gespenstisch.
12 **to quieten:** beruhigen.
25 **to make a mess of s.th.:** etwas verpfuschen.

 1 müde, erschöpft (anstrengend)

"I do not think anything would have been said to me about it if the person in whose possession it is was not prepared to sell it."

"Who's got it?"

"The Chinese woman who was living in Hammond's house."

A spot of colour flickered for an instant on Leslie's cheek-bones.

"Does she want an awful lot for it?"

"I imagine that she has a very shrewd idea of its value. I doubt if it would be possible to get hold of it except for a very large sum."

"Are you going to let me be hanged?"

"Do you think it's so simple as all that to secure possession of an unwelcome piece of evidence? It's no different from suborning a witness. You have no right to make any such suggestion to me."

"Then what is going to happen to me?"

"Justice must take its course."

She grew very pale. A little shudder passed through her body.

"I put myself in your hands. Of course I have no right to ask you to do anything that isn't proper."

Mr. Joyce had not bargained for the little break in her voice which her habitual self-restraint made quite intolerably moving. She looked at him with humble eyes, and

14f. **to secure possession:** sich des Besitzes versichern.
16 **to suborn a witness:** einen Zeugen zu falscher Aussage verleiten.
20 **shudder:** Schauer, Beben.
23 **proper:** schicklich; korrekt.
24 **to bargain for s.th.:** mit etwas rechnen.
25 **self-restraint:** Selbstbeherrschung.
26 **moving:** rührend, bewegend.

he thought that if he rejected their appeal they would haunt him for the rest of his life. After all, nothing could bring poor Hammond back to life again. He wondered what really was the explanation of that letter. It was not fair to conclude from it that she had killed Hammond without provocation. He had lived in the East a long time and his sense of professional honour was not perhaps so acute as it had been twenty years before. He stared at the floor. He made up his mind to do something which he knew was unjustifiable, but it stuck in his throat and he felt dully resentful towards Leslie. It embarrassed him a little to speak.

"I don't know exactly what your husband's circumstances are."

Flushing a rosy red, she shot a swift glance at him.

"He has a good many tin shares and a small share in two or three rubber estates. I suppose he could raise money."

"He would have to be told what it was for."

She was silent for a moment. She seemed to think.

"He's in love with me still. He would make any sacrifice to save me. Is there any need for him to see the letter?"

Mr. Joyce frowned a little, and, quick to notice, she went on.

1 **to reject:** abweisen.
appeal: (dringende) Bitte, Appell.
2 **to haunt:** heimsuchen, verfolgen.
8 **acute:** hier: geschärft.
11 **dully** (adv.): hier: dunkel, unbestimmt.
resentful: ärgerlich; grollend.
to embarrass: verlegen machen.
15 **to flush:** erröten.
16 **tin shares:** Zinn-Aktien.
17 f. **to raise money:** Geld aufbringen.

"Robert is an old friend of yours. I'm not asking you to do anything for me, I'm asking you to save a rather simple, kind man who never did you any harm from all the pain that's possible."

Mr. Joyce did not reply. He rose to go and Mrs. Crosbie, with the grace that was natural to her, held out her hand. She was shaken by the scene, and her look was haggard, but she made a brave attempt to speed him with courtesy.

"It's so good of you to take all this trouble for me. I can't begin to tell you how grateful I am."

Mr. Joyce returned to his office. He sat in his own room, quite still, attempting to do no work, and pondered. His imagination brought him many strange ideas. He shuddered a little. At last there was the discreet knock on the door which he was expecting. Ong Chi Seng came in.

"I was just going out to have my tiffin, sir," he said.

"All right."

"I didn't know if there was anything you wanted before I went, sir."

"I don't think so. Did you make another appointment for Mr. Reed?"

"Yes, sir. He will come at three o'clock."

"Good."

Ong Chi Seng turned away, walked to the door, and put

8 **to speed:** hier: verabschieden.
8f. **courtesy:** Höflichkeit.
13 **to ponder:** grübeln.
15 **to shudder:** schaudern; erbeben.
discreet: diskret.
18 **tiffin:** Mittagsmahl.

his long slim fingers on the handle. Then, as though on an afterthought, he turned back.

"Is there anything you wish me to say to my friend, sir?"

Although Ong Chi Seng spoke English so admirably he had still a difficulty with the letter R, and he pronounced it 'fliend'.

"What friend?"

"About the letter Mrs. Crosbie wrote to Hammond deceased, sir."

"Oh! I'd forgotten about that. I mentioned it to Mrs. Crosbie and she denies having written anything of the sort. It's evidently a forgery."

Mr. Joyce took the copy from his pocket and handed it to Ong Chi Seng. Ong Chi Seng ignored the gesture.

"In that case, sir, I suppose there would be no objection if my fliend delivered the letter to the Deputy Public Prosecutor."

"None. But I don't quite see what good that would do your friend."

"My fliend, sir, thought it was his duty in the interests of justice."

"I am the last man in the world to interfere with anyone who wishes to do his duty, Chi Seng."

The eyes of the lawyer and of the Chinese clerk met. Not the shadow of a smile hovered on the lips of either, but they understood each other perfectly.

"I quite understand, sir," said Ong Chi Seng, "but from my study of the case R. *v.* Crosbie I am of opinion that

1 **slim:** schlank.
2 **afterthought:** nachträglicher Einfall.
23 **to interfere:** sich einmischen.

the production of such a letter would be damaging to our client."
"I have always had a very high opinion of your legal acumen, Chi Seng."
"It has occurred to me, sir, that if I could persuade my fliend to induce the Chinese woman who has the letter to deliver it into our hands it would save a great deal of trouble."
Mr. Joyce idly drew faces on his blotting-paper.
"I suppose your friend is a business man. In what circumstances do you think he would be induced to part with the letter?"
"He has not got the letter. The Chinese woman has the letter. He is only a relation of the Chinese woman. She is an ignorant woman; she did not know the value of that letter till my fliend told her."
"What value did he put on it?"
"Ten thousand dollars, sir."
"Good God! Where on earth do you suppose Mrs. Crosbie can get ten thousand dollars! I tell you the letter's a forgery."
He looked up at Ong Chi Seng as he spoke. The clerk was unmoved by the outburst. He stood at the side of the desk, civil, cool and observant.

1 **production:** hier: Beibringen, Vorlage.
damaging: abträglich; schädlich.
4 **acumen:** Scharfsinn.
6 **to induce:** veranlassen, bewegen.
9 **idly** (adv.): hier: ziellos, planlos.
blotting-paper: Löschpapier.
11 f. **to part with s.th.:** sich von etwas trennen.
23 **outburst:** Ausbruch.
24 **civil:** höflich.
observant: beobachtend.

"Mr. Crosbie owns an eighth share of the Betong Rubber Estate and a sixth share of the Selantan River Rubber Estate. I have a fliend who will lend him the money on the security of his property."

"You have a large circle of acquaintance, Chi Seng."

"Yes, sir."

"Well, you can tell them all to go to hell. I would never advise Mr. Crosbie to give a penny more than five thousand for a letter that can be very easily explained."

"The Chinese woman does not want to sell the letter, sir. My fliend took a long time to persuade her. It is useless to offer her less than the sum mentioned."

Mr. Joyce looked at Ong Chi Seng for at least three minutes. The clerk bore the searching scrutiny without embarrassment. He stood in a respectful attitude with downcast eyes. Mr. Joyce knew his man. Clever fellow, Chi Seng, he thought, I wonder how much he's going to get out of it.

"Ten thousand dollars is a very large sum."

"Mr. Crosbie will certainly pay it rather than see his wife hanged, sir."

Again Mr. Joyce paused. What more did Chi Seng know than he had said? He must be pretty sure of his ground if he was obviously so unwilling to bargain. That sum had been fixed because whoever it was that was managing the

3 f. **on the security of his property:** mit seinem Eigentum als Sicherheit.
15 **searching:** forschend.
scrutiny: Untersuchung; prüfender Blick.
16 **embarrassment:** Verlegenheit.
respectful: ehrerbietig.
25 **to bargain:** handeln, feilschen.

affair knew it was the largest amount that Robert Crosbie could raise.

"Where is the Chinese woman now?" asked Mr. Joyce.

"She is staying at the house of my fliend, sir."

"Will she come here?"

"I think it more better if you go to her, sir. I can take you to the house to-night and she will give you the letter. She is a very ignorant woman, sir, and she does not understand cheques."

"I wasn't thinking of giving her a cheque. I will bring bank-notes with me."

"It would only be waste of valuable time to bring less than ten thousand dollars, sir."

"I quite understand."

"I will go and tell my fliend after I have had my tiffin, sir."

"Very good. You'd better meet me outside the club at ten o'clock to-night."

"With pleasure, sir," said Ong Chi Seng.

He gave Mr. Joyce a little bow and left the room. Mr. Joyce went out to have luncheon, too. He went to the club and here, as he had expected, he saw Robert Crosbie. He was sitting at a crowded table, and as he passed him, looking for a place, Mr. Joyce touched him on the shoulder.

"I'd like a word or two with you before you go," he said.

"Right you are. Let me know when you're ready."

Mr. Joyce had made up his mind how to tackle him. He

9 **cheque:** Scheck.
12 **waste:** Verschwendung.
21 **luncheon:** Mittagessen.
28 **to tackle s.o.:** jdn. angehen.

played a rubber of bridge after luncheon in order to allow time for the club to empty itself. He did not want on this particular matter to see Crosbie in his office. Presently Crosbie came into the card-room and looked on till the game was finished. The other players went on their various affairs, and the two were left alone.

"A rather unfortunate thing has happened, old man," said Mr. Joyce, in a tone which he sought to render as casual as possible. "It appears that your wife sent a letter to Hammond asking him to come to the bungalow on the night he was killed."

"But that's impossible," cried Crosbie. "She's always stated that she had had no communication with Hammond. I know from my own knowledge that she hadn't set eyes on him for a couple of months."

"The fact remains that the letter exists. It's in the possession of the Chinese woman Hammond was living with. Your wife meant to give you a present on your birthday, and she wanted Hammond to help her to get it. In the emotional excitement that she suffered from after the tragedy, she forgot all about it, and having once denied having any communication with Hammond she was afraid to say that she had made a mistake. It was, of course, very unfortunate, but I dare say it was not unnatural."

Crosbie did not speak. His large, red face bore an expression of complete bewilderment, and Mr. Joyce was at once relieved and exasperated by his lack of comprehension. He was a stupid man, and Mr. Joyce had no pa-

1 **rubber of bridge:** eine Art Bridgespiel.
27 **bewilderment:** Verstörtheit.
28 **exasperated:** verärgert.
28 f. **comprehension:** Verständnis.

tience with stupidity. But his distress since the catastrophe had touched a soft spot in the lawyer's heart; and Mrs. Crosbie had struck the right note when she asked him to help her, not for her sake, but for her husband's.

"I need not tell you that it would be very awkward if this letter found its way into the hands of the prosecution. Your wife has lied, and she would be asked to explain the lie. It alters things a little if Hammond did not intrude, an unwanted guest, but came to your house by invitation. It would be easy to arouse in the assessors a certain indecision of mind."

Mr. Joyce hesitated. He was face to face now with his decision. If it had been a time for humour, he could have smiled at the reflection that he was taking so grave a step, and that the man for whom he was taking it had not the smallest conception of its gravity. If he gave the matter a thought, he probably imagined that what Mr. Joyce was doing was what any lawyer did in the ordinary run of business.

"My dear Robert, you are not only my client, but my friend. I think we must get hold of that letter. It'll cost a good deal of money. Except for that I should have preferred to say nothing to you about it."

"How much?"

"Ten thousand dollars."

"That's a devil of a lot. With the slump and one thing and another it'll take just about all I've got."

3 **to strike the right note:** den richtigen Ton treffen.
5 **awkward:** hier: peinlich, unangenehm.
8 **to intrude:** eindringen.
10f. **indecision:** Unentschlossenheit.
16 **conception:** Vorstellung.
26 **slump:** Preissturz; Preisverfall.
26f. **one thing and another:** dies und jenes.

Qual, Not, Bedrängnis

"Can you get it at once?"

"I suppose so. Old Charlie Meadows will let me have it on my tin shares and on those two estates I'm interested in."

"Then will you?"

"Is it absolutely necessary?"

"If you want your wife to be acquitted."

Crosbie grew very red. His mouth sagged strangely.

"But . . ." He could not find words, his face now was purple. "But I don't understand. She can explain. You don't mean to say they'd find her guilty? They couldn't hang her for putting a noxious vermin out of the way."

"Of course they wouldn't hang her. They might only find her guilty of manslaughter. She'd probably get off with two or three years."

Crosbie started to his feet and his red face was distraught with horror.

"Three years."

Then something seemed to dawn in that slow intelligence of his. His mind was darkness across which shot suddenly a flash of lightning, and though the succeeding darkness was as profound, there remained the memory of something not seen but perhaps just descried. Mr. Joyce saw that Crosbie's big red hands, coarse and hard with all the odd jobs he had set them to, trembled.

7 **to acquit:** freisprechen.
8 **to sag:** sich nach unten verziehen.
14 **manslaughter:** Totschlag.
16 **to start to one's feet:** aufspringen.
19 **to dawn:** dämmern.
22 **profound:** tief(gründig).
23 **to descry:** wahrnehmen.
24 **coarse:** grob, rauh.
25 **odd jobs:** Gelegenheitsarbeiten.

"What was the present she wanted to make me?"
"She says she wanted to give you a new gun."
Once more that great red face flushed a deeper red.
"When have you got to have the money ready?"
There was something odd in his voice now. It sounded as though he spoke with invisible hands clutching at his throat.
"At ten o'clock to-night. I thought you could bring it to my office at about six."
"Is the woman coming to you?"
"No, I'm going to her."
"I'll bring the money. I'll come with you."
Mr. Joyce looked at him sharply.
"Do you think there's any need for you to do that? I think it would be better if you left me to deal with this matter by myself."
"It's my money, isn't it? I'm going to come."
Mr. Joyce shrugged his shoulders. They rose and shook hands. Mr. Joyce looked at him curiously.
At ten o'clock they met in the empty club.
"Everything all right?" asked Mr. Joyce.
"Yes. I've got the money in my pocket."
"Let's go then."
They walked down the steps. Mr. Joyce's car was waiting for them in the square, silent at that hour, and as they came to it Ong Chi Seng stepped out of the shadow of a house. He took his seat beside the driver and gave him a direction. They drove past the Hotel de l'Europe and turned up by the Sailor's Home to get into Victoria Street. Here the Chinese shops were still open, idlers

6 **to clutch:** packen.
30 **idler:** Müßiggänger.

lounged about, and in the roadway rickshaws and motor-cars and gharries gave a busy air to the scene. Suddenly their car stopped and Chi Seng turned round.
"I think it more better if we walk here, sir," he said. They got out and he went on. They followed a step or two behind. Then he asked them to stop.
"You wait here, sir. I go in and speak to my fliend."
He went into a shop, open to the street, where three or four Chinese were standing behind the counter. It was one of those strange shops where nothing was on view, and you wondered what it was they sold there. They saw him address a stout man in a duck suit with a large gold chain across his breast, and the man shot a quick glance out into the night. He gave Chi Seng a key and Chi Seng came out. He beckoned to the two men waiting and slid into a doorway at the side of the shop. They followed him and found themselves at the foot of a flight of stairs.
"If you wait a minute I will light a match," he said, always resourceful. "You come upstairs, please."
He held a Japanese match in front of them, but it scarcely dispelled the darkness and they groped their way up

1 **to lounge about:** herumbummeln.
roadway: Fahrbahn.
2 **gharry:** kleine Pferdekutsche.
air: Aussehen.
9 **counter:** Ladentisch.
12 **to address s.o.:** jdn. anreden; sich an jdn. wenden.
stout: untersetzt.
duck suit: Leinenanzug.
15 **to beckon to s.o.:** jdm. zunicken, zuwinken.
16 **doorway:** Hauseingang, -einfahrt.
17 **flight of stairs:** Treppenhaus.
19 **resourceful:** findig, erfinderisch.
21 **to dispel:** vertreiben.
to grope: tasten.

behind him. On the first floor he unlocked a door and going in lit a gas-jet.
"Come in, please," he said.
It was a small square room, with one window, and the only furniture consisted of two low Chinese beds covered with matting. In one corner was a large chest, with an elaborate lock, and on this stood a shabby tray with an opium pipe on it and a lamp. There was in the room the faint, acrid scent of the drug. They sat down and Ong Chi Seng offered them cigarettes. In a moment the door was opened by the fat Chinaman whom they had seen behind the counter. He bade them good-evening in very good English, and sat down by the side of his fellow-countryman.
"The Chinese woman is just coming," said Chi Seng.
A boy from the shop brought in a tray with a teapot and cups and the Chinaman offered them a cup of tea. Crosbie refused. The Chinese talked to one another in undertones, but Crosbie and Mr. Joyce were silent. At last there was the sound of a voice outside; someone was calling in a low tone; and the Chinaman went to the door. He opened it, spoke a few words, and ushered a woman in. Mr. Joyce looked at her. He had heard much about her since Hammond's death, but he had never seen her. She was a stoutish person, not very young, with a broad,

2 **gas-jet:** Gaslampe.
6 **matting:** Mattenbelag, Mattenstoff.
7 **elaborate:** hier: kompliziert.
shabby: schäbig.
tray: Tablett.
9 **acrid:** beißend, scharf.
scent: Geruch.
22 **to usher s.o. in:** jdn. hineingeleiten.
25 **stoutish:** etwas untersetzt.

phlegmatic face, she was powdered and rouged and her eyebrows were a thin black line, but she gave you the impression of a woman of character. She wore a pale blue jacket and a white skirt, her costume was not quite European nor quite Chinese, but on her feet were little Chinese silk slippers. She wore heavy gold chains round her neck, gold bangles on her wrists, gold ear-rings and elaborate gold pins in her black hair. She walked in slowly, with the air of a woman sure of herself, but with a certain heaviness of tread, and sat down on the bed beside Ong Chi Seng. He said something to her and nodding she gave an incurious glance at the two white men.

"Has she got the letter?" asked Mr. Joyce.

"Yes, sir."

Crosbie said nothing, but produced a roll of five-hundred-dollar notes. He counted out twenty and handed them to Chi Seng.

"Will you see if that is correct?"

The clerk counted them and gave them to the fat Chinaman.

"Quite correct, sir."

The Chinaman counted them once more and put them in his pocket. He spoke again to the woman and she drew from her bosom a letter. She gave it to Chi Seng who cast his eyes over it.

"This is the right document, sir," he said, and was about to give it to Mr. Joyce when Crosbie took it from him.

1 **rouged:** rot geschminkt.
7 **bangle:** Armreif.
10 **tread:** Tritt, Schritt.
12 **incurious:** teilnahmslos.

"Let me look at it," he said.

Mr. Joyce watched him read and then held out his hand for it.

"You'd better let me have it."

Crosbie folded it up deliberately and put it in his pocket.

"No, I'm going to keep it myself. It's cost me enough money."

Mr. Joyce made no rejoinder. The three Chinese watched the little passage, but what they thought about it, or whether they thought, it was impossible to tell from their impassive countenances. Mr. Joyce rose to his feet.

"Do you want me any more to-night, sir?" said Ong Chi Seng.

"No." He knew that the clerk wished to stay behind in order to get his agreed share of the money, and he turned to Crosbie. "Are you ready?"

Crosbie did not answer, but stood up. The Chinaman went to the door and opened it for them. Chi Seng found a bit of candle and lit it in order to light them down, and the two Chinese accompanied them to the street. They left the woman sitting quietly on the bed smoking a cigarette. When they reached the street the Chinese left them and went once more upstairs.

"What are you going to do with that letter?" asked Mr. Joyce.

"Keep it."

They walked to where the car was waiting for them and

8 **rejoinder:** Erwiderung.
9 **passage:** hier: Geschäftsvorgang, Transaktion.
11 **impassive:** unbewegt, unbeweglich; teilnahmslos.
16 **his agreed share:** sein vereinbarter Anteil.

here Mr. Joyce offered his friend a lift. Crosbie shook his head.

"I'm going to walk." He hesitated a little and shuffled his feet. "I went to Singapore on the night of Hammond's death partly to buy a new gun that a man I knew wanted to dispose of. Good-night."

He disappeared quickly into the darkness.

Mr. Joyce was quite right about the trial. The assessors went into court fully determined to acquit Mrs. Crosbie. She gave evidence on her own behalf. She told her story simply and with straightforwardness. The D. P. P. was a kindly man and it was plain that he took no great pleasure in his task. He asked the necessary questions in a deprecating manner. His speech for the prosecution might really have been a speech for the defence, and the assessors took less than five minutes to consider their popular verdict. It was impossible to prevent the great outburst of applause with which it was received by the crowd that packed the court-house. The judge congratulated Mrs. Crosbie and she was a free woman.

No one had expressed a more violent disapprobation of Hammond's behaviour than Mrs. Joyce; she was a woman loyal to her friends and she had insisted on the Crosbies staying with her after the trial, for she in common with everyone else had no doubt of the result, till they could make arrangements to go away. It was out of

1 **to offer s.o. a lift:** jdm. anbieten, ihn (im Auto) mitzunehmen.
3f. **to shuffle one's feet:** mit den Füßen scharren.
6 **to dispose of s.th.:** etwas abstoßen, sich einer Sache entledigen.
10 **to give evidence on one's own behalf:** in eigener Sache aussagen.
11 **straightforwardness:** Ehrlichkeit.
D. P. P.: Abk. für *Deputy Public Prosecutor.*
13f. **deprecating:** mißbilligend.
21 **disapprobation:** Mißbilligung.

the question for poor, dear, brave Leslie to return to the bungalow at which the horrible catastrophe had taken place. The trial was over by half-past twelve and when they reached the Joyces' house a grand luncheon was awaiting them. Cocktails were ready, Mrs. Joyce's million-dollar cocktail was celebrated through all the Malay States, and Mrs. Joyce drank Leslie's health. She was a talkative, vivacious woman, and now she was in the highest spirits. It was fortunate, for the rest of them were silent. She did not wonder; her husband never had much to say, and the other two were naturally exhausted from the long strain to which they had been subjected. During luncheon she carried on a bright and spirited monologue. Then coffee was served.

"Now, children," she said in her gay, bustling fashion, "you must have a rest and after tea I shall take you both for a drive to the sea."

Mr. Joyce, who lunched at home only by exception, had of course to go back to his office.

"I'm afraid I can't do that, Mrs. Joyce," said Crosbie. "I've got to get back to the estate at once."

"Not to-day?" she cried.

"Yes, now. I've neglected it for too long and I have urgent business. But I shall be very grateful if you will keep Leslie until we have decided what to do."

Mrs. Joyce was about to expostulate, but her husband prevented her.

8 **talkative:** geschwätzig.
vivacious: lebhaft.
12 **strain:** Anstrengung, Strapaze.
13 **spirited:** geistvoll; lebhaft.
15 **bustling:** geschäftig.
26 **to expostulate:** Vorhaltungen machen; Einwände erheben.

"If he must go, he must, and there's an end of it."
There was something in the lawyer's tone which made her look at him quickly. She held her tongue and there was a moment's silence. Then Crosbie spoke again.
"If you'll forgive me, I'll start at once so that I can get there before dark." He rose from the table. "Will you come and see me off, Leslie?"
"Of course."
They went out of the dining-room together.
"I think that's rather inconsiderate of him," said Mrs. Joyce. "He must know that Leslie wants to be with him just now."
"I'm sure he wouldn't go if it wasn't absolutely necessary."
"Well, I'll just see that Leslie's room is ready for her. She wants a complete rest, of course, and then amusement."
Mrs. Joyce left the room and Joyce sat down again. In a short time he heard Crosbie start the engine of his motorcycle and then noisily scrunch over the gravel of the garden path. He got up and went into the drawing-room. Mrs. Crosbie was standing in the middle of it, looking into space, and in her hand was an open letter. He recognised it. She gave him a glance as he came in and he saw that she was deathly pale.
"He knows," she whispered.
Mr. Joyce went up to her and took the letter from her hand. He lit a match and set the paper afire. She watched it burn. When he could hold it no longer he dropped it on

7 **to see s.o. off:** jdn. wegbegleiten.
10 **inconsiderate:** unbedacht, gedankenlos.
20 **to scrunch:** knirschen; knirschend fahren.

the tiled floor and they both looked at the paper curl and blacken. Then he trod it into ashes with his foot.

"What does he know?"

She gave him a long, long stare and into her eyes came a strange look. Was it contempt or despair? Mr. Joyce could not tell.

"He knows that Geoff. was my lover."

Mr. Joyce made no movement and uttered no sound.

"He'd been my lover for years. He became my lover almost immediately after he came back from the war. We knew how careful we must be. When we became lovers I pretended I was tired of him, and he seldom came to the house when Robert was there. I used to drive out to a place we knew and he met me, two or three times a week, and when Robert went to Singapore he used to come to the bungalow late, when the boys had gone for the night. We saw one another constantly, all the time, and not a soul had the smallest suspicion of it. And then lately, a year ago, he began to change. I didn't know what was the matter. I couldn't believe that he didn't care for me any more. He always denied it. I was frantic. I made him scenes. Sometimes I thought he hated me. Oh, if you knew what agonies I endured. I passed through hell. I knew he didn't want me any more and I wouldn't let him go. Misery! Misery! I loved him. I'd given him everything. He was my life. And then I heard he was living with a Chinese woman. I couldn't believe it. I wouldn't believe it. At last I saw her, I saw her with my own eyes,

1 **tiled:** gefliest.
5 **contempt:** Verachtung.
12 **to pretend:** vorgeben.
23 **agony:** Pein; Qual.
to endure: leiden.

walking in the village, with her gold bracelets and her necklaces, an old, fat, Chinese woman. She was older than I was. Horrible! They all knew in the kampong that she was his mistress. And when I passed her, she looked at me and I knew that she knew I was his mistress too. I sent for him. I told him I must see him. You've read the letter. I was mad to write it. I didn't know what I was doing. I didn't care. I hadn't seen him for ten days. It was a lifetime. And when last we'd parted he took me in his arms and kissed me, and told me not to worry. And he went straight from my arms to hers."

She had been speaking in a low voice, vehemently, and now she stopped and wrung her hands.

"That damned letter. We'd always been so careful. He always tore up any word I wrote to him the moment he'd read it. How was I to know he'd leave that one? He came, and I told him I knew about the Chinawoman. He denied it. He said it was only scandal. I was beside myself. I don't know what I said to him. Oh, I hated him then. I tore him limb from limb. I said everything I could to wound him. I insulted him. I could have spat in his face. And at last he turned on me. He told me he was sick and tired of me and never wanted to see me again. He said I bored him to death. And then he acknowledged that it

1 **bracelet:** Armreif.
3 **kampong:** (Eingeborenen-)Dorf.
4 **mistress:** Geliebte.
8 f. **It was a lifetime:** etwa: Es war eine Ewigkeit.
13 **to wring one's hands:** die Hände ringen.
18 **scandal:** üble Nachrede, Verleumdung.
19 f. **I tore him limb from limb:** etwa: Ich zerriß ihn in der Luft.
22 **to turn on s.o.:** sich von jdm. abwenden.
24 **to acknowledge:** hier: eingestehen.

Halskette

was true about the Chinawoman. He said he'd known her for years, before the war, and she was the only woman who really meant anything to him, and the rest was just pastime. And he said he was glad I knew and now at last I'd leave him alone. And then I don't know what happened, I was beside myself, I saw red. I seized the revolver and I fired. He gave a cry and I saw I'd hit him. He staggered and rushed for the verandah. I ran after him and fired again. He fell and then I stood over him and I fired and fired till the revolver went click, click, and I knew there were no more cartridges."

At last she stopped, panting. Her face was no longer human, it was distorted with cruelty, and rage and pain. You would never have thought that this quiet, refined woman was capable of such fiendish passion. Mr. Joyce took a step backwards. He was absolutely aghast at the sight of her. It was not a face, it was a gibbering, hideous mask. Then they heard a voice calling from another room, a loud, friendly, cheerful voice. It was Mrs. Joyce.

"Come along, Leslie darling, your room's ready. You must be dropping with sleep."

Mrs. Crosbie's features gradually composed themselves. Those passions, so clearly delineated, were smoothed

4 **pastime:** Zeitvertreib.
11 **cartridge:** Patrone.
13 **distorted:** verzerrt.
15 **fiendish:** teuflisch.
16 **aghast:** entgeistert.
18 **hideous:** abscheulich.
23 **to compose o.s.:** sich beruhigen; sich fassen.
24 **to delineate:** abzeichnen.
24 f. **to smooth away:** glatt streichen.

away as with your hand you would smooth a crumpled paper, and in a minute the face was cool and calm and unlined. She was a trifle pale, but her lips broke into a pleasant, affable smile. She was once more the well-bred and even distinguished woman.

"I'm coming, Dorothy dear. I'm sorry to give you so much trouble."

3 **unlined:** faltenlos.
4 **affable:** freundlich.
well-bred: wohlerzogen.

Editorische Notiz

Der englische Text folgt der Ausgabe: W. Somerset Maugham, *The Complete Short Stories*, Bd. 3, London: Heinemann, 1951, S. 1414–45. Das Glossar erklärt in der Regel alle Wörter, die über die Wertigkeitsstufe 4 des *Englischen Arbeitswörterbuches* von Alfred Haase (Frankfurt a. M.: Moritz Diesterweg, ^{7}1979) hinausgehen. Im Zweifelsfall wurde großzügig verfahren, d. h. eher eine Vokabel mehr aufgenommen als dort vorgesehen.

Im Glossar verwendete Abkürzungen

adv.	adverb
coll.	colloquial (umgangssprachlich)
fig.	figuratively (übertragen)
frz.	französisch
o.s.	oneself
pej.	pejorative (abwertend, verächtlich)
pl.	plural
s.o.	someone
s.th.	something

Literaturhinweise

Ausgaben

The Collected Edition of the Works of W. Somerset Maugham, London: Heinemann, 1928–59.
The Complete Short Stories, 3 Bde., London: Heinemann, 1951 [u. ö.].
The Casuarina Tree. Six Stories, London: Heinemann, 1953.

The Summing Up, London: Heinemann, 1938, Repr. Garden City, N. Y., 1950.
A Writer's Notebook, London: Heinemann, 1949.

Sekundärliteratur

Brophy, John, *Somerset Maugham*, London 1952 [u. ö.].
Brown, Ivor, *W. Somerset Maugham*, London 1970.
Calder, Robert Lorin, *W. Somerset Maugham and the Quest for Freedom*, London 1972.
Cordell, Richard A., *Somerset Maugham: A Biographical and Critical Study*, Bloomington 1961.
Curtis, Anthony, *The Pattern of Maugham*, London 1974.
Jonas, Klaus W. (Hrsg.), *The Maugham Enigma. An Anthology*, London 1954.
– (Hrsg.), *The World of Somerset Maugham. An Anthology*, New York 1959.
Kanin, Garson, *Remembering Mr. Maugham*, New York 1966.
Maugham, Robin, *Somerset and All the Maughams*, London 1966.
– *Conversations with Willie*, London 1978.
Nichols, Beverley, *A Case of Human Bondage*, London 1966.
Pfeiffer, Karl G., *Somerset Maugham: A Candid Portrait*, New York 1959.
Raphael, Frederic, *Somerset Maugham and his World*, London 1976.

Stott, Raymond Toole, *Maughamiana: The Writings of W. Somerset Maugham*, London 1964. [Ein Verzeichnis aller Werke W. Somerset Maughams einschl. Zeitschriftenartikel.]

Nachwort

William Somerset Maugham wurde 1874 in Paris geboren. Sein Vater diente der Britischen Botschaft als »solicitor« und betrieb gleichzeitig ein privates Anwaltsbüro; seine Mutter, kunstsinnig und einer alten englischen Familie entstammend, führte im Paris des ausgehenden 19. Jahrhunderts einen literarischen Salon, dessen Besucher solch illustre Namen wie Prosper Mérimée und Gustave Doré trugen.

So wuchs der kleine Willie wohlbehütet in einem eleganten Haus unweit der Champs-Elysées auf; Französisch war seine eigentliche Muttersprache, in der er sich auch mit seinen Eltern und Brüdern unterhielt. Das Englische lernte er zunächst eher nebenher wie eine Fremdsprache. Französischer Sprache und Kultur hat Maugham sich stets auf das engste verbunden gefühlt:

> »It was France that educated me, France that taught me to value beauty, distinction, wit and good sense, France that taught me to write. I have spent many happy years in France.«[1]

1882 starb seine Mutter, zwei Jahre später sein Vater. Nun, im Alter von zehn Jahren, erlebte Maugham den wohl folgenschwersten Einschnitt seines Lebens: er wurde von seinen Brüdern getrennt und der Erziehung seines Patenonkels, eines Geistlichen in Whitstable in Kent, anvertraut. Aus der Metropole Paris verschlug es ihn so in ein viktorianisches Provinzstädtchen; sein Englisch, weit davon entfernt, vollkommen zu sein, stempelte ihn zum »alien«. Er mußte sein weltoffenes, wohlhabendes Elternhaus mit dem puritanisch strengen, eher ärmlichen Pfarrhaus tauschen, in dem ein bigotter »vicar« tyrannisch herrschte. Zudem stotterte Maugham zeit seines Lebens: all diese Umstände drängten ihn in die Rolle des in sich gekehrten, schüchternen Außenseiters:

1 W. Somerset Maugham, *A Writer's Notebook*, London 1949, S. 278.

Rechtsbeistand, Anwalt, Agent

»I had many disabilities. I was small; I had endurance but little physical strength; I stammered; I was shy; I had poor health.«[2]

Seine Schulzeit in der King's School zu Cambridge durchlitt er wie ein Fegefeuer, von Mitschülern und auch Lehrern ständig wegen seines Sprachfehlers gehänselt. In seinem wohl bekanntesten Roman *Of Human Bondage* (1915) hat er seine Jugendjahre halb-autobiographisch verarbeitet; die vermeintliche Roheit und Brutalität des Onkels ist indes stark überzeichnet, wie Maugham in späteren Jahren selbst einräumte.

Wegen seines Sprachfehlers war ihm die der Familientradition gemäße juristische Karriere verstellt (einer seiner Brüder avancierte später zum Lord Chancellor); Maugham entschied sich fürs Medizinstudium, das er nach den sieben freudlosen, seinen Freiheitsdrang einengenden Jahren der Schulzeit endlich in der Hauptstadt London aufnahm. Ein Jahr seiner Studien verbrachte er in Heidelberg; dort ließ ihn der Kontakt mit der deutschen Philosophie zum Agnostiker werden. In Heidelberg reifte auch sein Entschluß, die Laufbahn eines Schriftstellers einzuschlagen, doch hat er seine medizinische Ausbildung stets als eine hervorragende Grundlage für seine spätere Karriere angesehen:

»I do not know a better training for a writer than to spend some years in the medical profession [. . .]. The doctor sees human nature bare [. . .]. The doctor is discreet. It is his business to listen, and no details are too intimate for his ears.«[3]

Als junger Arzt empfing er auch die Eindrücke, die seinem ersten bedeutenden Werk, dem Roman *Liza of Lambeth* (1897), zugrunde liegen; dieses Werk steht noch ganz in der naturalistischen Tradition eines Maupassant oder Zola.

In der Absicht, seinen Erlebnishorizont zu erweitern, unternahm Maugham bald ausgedehnte Reisen nach Spanien, Italien und immer wieder Frankreich. In den Jahren vor dem Ersten Weltkrieg war er der erfolgreichste Dramatiker auf den Londo-

2 W. Somerset Maugham, *The Summing Up*, London 1938, S. 34.
3 Ebd., S. 45.

ner Bühnen. Sein erstes Stück mit dem deutschen Titel *Schiffbrüchig* hatte er schon im Alter von 18 Jahren verfaßt; erst jetzt gelang ihm mit wiewohl recht konventionellen, von Shaw und Ibsen beeinflußten Gesellschaftskomödien wie *Lady Frederick* (1912) und *Jack Straw* (1912) auch in dieser Gattung der Durchbruch. Maugham war nun so überaus erfolgreich und wohlhabend geworden, daß er es sich in den zwanziger Jahren leisten konnte, dem Theater zunächst seinen Dienst aufzukündigen und sich wieder der in seinen Augen seriöseren, mehr Freiraum gewährenden Epik zu widmen:

> »I sighed for the liberty of fiction, and thought with pleasure of the lonely reader who was willing to listen to all I had to say and with whom I could effect an intimacy that I could never hope for in the garish publicity of the theatre [. . .]. I thought I would go while the going was good.«[4]

1916 heiratete er. Es war jedoch ein eher zwiespältiges Verhältnis, da Maugham gleichzeitig homosexuelle Verbindungen einging; so erkor er sich den etwas windigen Amerikaner Gerald Haxton zum Sekretär und Gefährten, der, weltgewandt und kontaktfreudig, Maugham manche der Stoffe zutrug, die dieser dann literarisch umsetzte. Aus dieser Quelle bezog Maugham auch die Vorlage zu *The Letter*.

Im Weltkrieg hatte Maugham als Agent des Secret Service gearbeitet; in den Jahren danach bereiste er fast die ganze Welt, vor allem Länder des Britischen Empire. Romane wie *The Moon and Sixpence* (1919) und *Cakes and Ale* (1930) wurzeln in diesen Reiseerlebnissen. Gleichzeitig war Maugham auch als Verfasser von Short Stories und Theaterstücken überaus produktiv. Geschäftstüchtig wie er war, verarbeitete er nicht selten denselben Stoff in verschiedenen Versionen (oder ließ das andere machen). Auch von *The Letter* existiert eine Bühnenfassung in drei Akten (1927), dazu noch eine Filmversion, in der allerdings gemäß den Moralvorstellungen von Hollywood die Mörderin ihrer gerechten Strafe zugeführt wird.

Seinen ständigen Wohnsitz hatte er längst an der Côte d'Azur

4 Ebd., S. 103 f.

genommen; als einer der wohlhabendsten Schriftsteller der Zeit konnte er es sich leisten, ein großes Haus zu führen und zahlreiche zeitgenössische Berühmtheiten gastfreundlich aufzunehmen. In den letzten Jahren seines Lebens – er starb 1965 – verfaßte Maugham vornehmlich literarische und zeitkritische Essays.

In allen drei Gattungen, in denen sich Maugham während einer Spanne von über fünfzig Jahren hervortat, also im Roman, in der Short Story sowie in der Gesellschaftskomödie, ist er stets vom Realismus und Positivismus des ausgehenden 19. Jahrhunderts geprägt geblieben, wenn er auch in der Themenwahl dem jeweiligen Zeitgeschmack folgte. Seine erzählerische Technik wandelte sich kaum, sie blieb weitgehend konventionell. Wie ein roter Faden zieht sich seine ätzende Kritik des Menschen (von manchen Kritikern als blanker Zynismus aufgefaßt) durch sein Werk: nicht moralische Maßstäbe, sondern Zufälle, Launen und physische Zwänge bestimmen die Handlungen des Menschen, so wie sie auch Maughams eigenes Leben prägten. Dabei bietet sich dem Beobachter der Mensch als zerrissenes, im tiefsten widersprüchliches Wesen:

> »I think what has chiefly struck me in human beings is their lack of consistency. I have never seen people all of a piece. It has amazed me that the most incongruous traits should exist in the same person and for all that yield a plausible harmony. I have often asked myself how characteristics, seemingly irreconcilable, can exist in the same person.«[5]

Aber erst durch Aufdeckung dieser Widersprüchlichkeiten erfährt man nach Maugham den Menschen in seinem wahren Wesen:

> »Selfishness and kindliness, idealism and sensuality, vanity, shyness, disinterestedness, courage, laziness, nervousness, obstinacy, and diffidence, they can all exist in a single person and form a plausible harmony. It has taken a long time to persuade readers of the truth of this.«[6]

Man darf nicht vergessen, daß die literarische Szene im England

5 Ebd., S. 40.
6 Ebd., S. 48.

des beginnenden 20. Jahrhunderts noch weithin viktorianisch-sentimentalistisch bestimmt war, so daß von Maughams Werk durchaus neue Impulse ausgingen. Autobiographische Romane sind in dieser Zeit nicht selten: Butlers *The Way of All Flesh* (1903) hat sicherlich *Of Human Bondage* thematisch beeinflußt; den literarischen Rang eines Werkes wie *Sons and Lovers* (1913) von D. H. Lawrence erreichte Maugham indes nie. Maugham blieb stets ein virtuoser, auf Effekt bedachter und technisch überaus kompetenter Schriftsteller, dem die fehlende Anerkennung vieler ernst zu nehmender Kritiker wohl nur scheinbar nichts ausmachte:

> »I have no illusions about my literary position. There are but two important critics in my own country who have troubled to take me seriously, and when clever young men write essays about contemporary fiction they never think of considering me. I do not resent it [. . .]. I look upon it as very natural that the world of letters should have attached no great importance to my work. In the drama I have found myself at home in the traditional moulds. As writer of fiction I go back, through innumerable generations, to the teller of tales round the fire in the cavern that sheltered neolithic men.«[7]

So wie sich im Drama hauptsächlich der Einfluß von Ibsen leicht nachweisen läßt, so ist in Maughams erzählenden Werken der französische Naturalismus – vor allem Maupassant – bestimmend gewesen. Maughams konventionelle Erzählweise kam dem Geschmack eines breiten Publikums entgegen; experimentelle Techniken verabscheute er:

> »I wanted to write stories that proceeded, tightly knit, in an unbroken line from the exposition to the conclusion. I saw the short story as a narrative of a single event, material or spiritual, to which by the elimination of everything that was not essential to its elucidation a dramatic unity could be given. I had no fear of what is technically known as ›the point‹ [. . .]. In short, I preferred to end my short stories with a full-stop rather than with a straggle of dots.«[8]

7 Ebd., S. 143 f.
8 Ebd., S. 138 f.

Viele seiner Romane und Short Stories basieren auf wirklichen Begebenheiten, die Maugham in seine künstlerischen Vorstellungen einpaßte. So liegt auch *The Letter* ein Ereignis zugrunde, das sich Anfang der zwanziger Jahre zutrug.
The Letter erschien zunächst 1924 in einer Zeitschrift, dann 1926 in der Sammlung *The Casuarina Tree*. Dieser Band enthielt – wie auch einige vorausgegangene Sammlungen – exotische Erzählungen. Nach den Schrecken des Weltkrieges war bei den Lesern ein eskapistisches Bedürfnis nach einer zumindest äußerlich intakten Welt entstanden. Im Mittelpunkt aller Erzählungen stehen Europäer, häufig Repräsentanten des niedergehenden britischen Kolonialreiches; die Eingeborenen mit ihrer Kultur, die exotische Landschaft bilden kaum mehr als Staffage, von der sich die Protagonisten um so schärfer abheben. Doch hat die exponierte Situation der Hauptcharaktere auch eine wichtige dramatische Funktion:

> »What excited me was to meet one person after another who was new to me. I was like a naturalist who comes into a country where the fauna are of an unimaginable variety [. . .]. In civilized communities men's idiosyncrasies are mitigated by the necessity of conforming to certain rules of behaviour. Culture is a mask that hides their faces. Here people showed themselves bare.«[9]

Darauf spielt auch der Titel *The Casuarina Tree* an. Maugham erklärte selbst im Vorwort zu dieser Sammlung:

> »[. . .] I remembered that the Casuarina Tree stood along the sea shore, gaunt and rough-hewn, protecting the land from the fury of the winds, and so might aptly suggest these planters and administrators who, with all their shortcomings, have after all brought to the peoples among whom they dwell tranquillity, justice and welfare, and I fancied that they too, as they looked at the Casuarina Tree, grey, rugged and sad, a little out of place in the wanton tropics, might very well be reminded of their native land [. . .].«[10]

9 Ebd., S. 131.
10 W. Somerset Maugham, *The Casuarina Tree*, London 1953, S. VIII.

The Letter fällt in dieser Sammlung insofern aus dem Rahmen, als die Hauptfigur Leslie Crosbie nicht oder nur indirekt eine Vertreterin des kolonialen Apparats ist; der britische Kolonialgeist, der z. B. *The Outstation* durchzieht, klingt nur im Hintergrund an und läßt uns *The Letter* weniger zeitgebunden erscheinen. Die aktuellen Bezüge waren eingeweihten Lesern indes offenkundig; der Kritiker Frederic Raphael schreibt:

> »›The Letter‹ was so scandalously *à clef* as to amount to a flagrant breach of hospitality and perhaps of good taste.«[11]

Maugham selbst zeigte sich davon ungerührt:

> »If the shoe fits, wear it.«[12]

Noch viele Jahre grollte man Maugham wegen *The Letter*:

> »In 1959 he made his last visit to the Far East. When he first published his stories about Malaya, indignant Colonials heaped anathemas on him. How could ›The Letter‹ ever be forgiven?«[13]

In *The Letter* lassen sich leicht Maughams Erfahrungen als Dramatiker aufzeigen: die Geschichte entfaltet sich in knappen dialogischen Szenen, die geradlinig ihrem Höhepunkt zustreben. Nicht nur das Thema des Mordes siedelt diese Short Story in der Nähe der Kriminalgeschichte an; der Leser wird fast unmerklich in die Irre geführt, indem der Blickpunkt der Leslie Crosbie schier bruchlos in den des Erzählers überzugehen scheint und so subjektive zur objektiven Schilderung wird. Auch in *The Letter* ist die Charakteranalyse zentral: wieder einmal beschreibt Maugham den Menschen in seiner Widersprüchlichkeit, wenn der Autor sich auch jeder moralisierenden Stellungnahme enthält:

> »I am not my brother's keeper. I cannot bring myself to judge my fellows; I am content to observe them. My observation has led me to believe that, all in all, there is not so much difference as the moralists would have us believe.«[14]

11 Frederic Raphael, *Somerset Maugham and his World*, London 1976, S. 62.

12 Zit. bei Richard A. Cordell, *Somerset Maugham: A Biographical and Critical Study*, Bloomington 1961, S. 119.

13 Raphael (Anm. 11) S. 110.

14 Maugham, *The Summing Up* (Anm. 2), S. 41.

Maughams sezierender, klinischer »approach« läßt die Schurken seiner Geschichten (wenn es sich nicht gerade um Eingeborene handelt) in der Regel ungeschoren davonkommen – »such is life«, so daß z. B. der Kritiker Cyril Connolly, der im übrigen Maugham für den größten zeitgenössischen Verfasser von Short Stories hielt, den chinesischen Erpresser Ong Chi Sen für den eigentlichen verwerflichen Charakter in *The Letter* ansieht. Leslie Crosbie ist so abgrundtief böse und verderbt, so ohne jede Reue und Mitgefühl, daß der Kritiker Anthony Curtis sie mit einer der eindrucksvollsten Shakespeare-Figuren vergleicht:

> »[. . .] she is a kind of Lady Macbeth who, unlike her illustrious archetype, suffers no remorse, no crack-up, no handwashing, but lives to enjoy the fruits of her crime in successful, hard-working tranquillity as a respected figure of the community.«[15]

Damit mag Maugham vielleicht die Regeln der poetischen Gerechtigkeit verletzen; daß seine Darstellungsweise umso eindringlicher ist, wer wollte es ernsthaft bestreiten?

Man hat Maugham gelegentlich allzu klischeehafter Erzähltechnik und eines kalten Professionalismus geziehen; sein jahrzehntelanger, nachhaltiger Erfolg in ganz unterschiedlichen Gattungen, seine Anziehungskraft auf »high brow«- und »low brow«-Leserschaft (gerade die letztere Gruppe mag durch Maugham häufig erst an Literatur herangeführt worden sein) lassen ihn als einen der ganz wichtigen, wenn auch nicht unumstrittenen englischen Autoren der ersten Hälfte unseres Jahrhunderts erscheinen.

Ulrich Hiller

15 Anthony Curtis, *The Pattern of Maugham*, London 1974, S. 163.

Inhalt

Fremdsprachentexte

IN RECLAMS UNIVERSAL-BIBLIOTHEK

Englisch

Lewis Carroll: Alice's Adventures in Wonderland. Mit Illustrationen von John Tenniel. Herausgegeben von Dietrich Klose. 9160 [2]

Joseph Conrad: Heart of Darkness. Herausgegeben von Bernhard Reitz. 9161 [2]

Charles Dickens: A Christmas Carol. Herausgegeben von Herbert Geisen. 9150 [2]

Arthur Conan Doyle: Silver Blaze. / The Sussex Vampire. Herausgegeben von Klaus Degering. 9170

Graham Greene: The Third Man. Herausgegeben von Bernd Lenz. 9180 [2]

James Joyce: Dubliners. A Selection. Herausgegeben von Harald Beck. 9181

Doris Lessing: To Room Nineteen. Herausgegeben von Günther Jarfe. 9151

Katherine Mansfield: The Garden-Party. Five Short Stories. Herausgegeben von Karin Friedmann. 9152

W. Somerset Maugham: The Letter. Herausgegeben von Ulrich Hiller. 9183

Arthur Miller: Death of a Salesman. Herausgegeben von Manfred und Gunda Pütz. 9172 [2]

Modern English Short Stories I: From Hardy to Maugham. Herausgegeben von Hans-Christian Oeser. 9184 [2]

Fremdsprachentexte

IN RECLAMS UNIVERSAL-BIBLIOTHEK

Französisch

Marcel Aymé: Le Passe-muraille et autres nouvelles. Herausgegeben von Ernst Kemmner. 9179

Honoré de Balzac: Le Colonel Chabert. Herausgegeben von Wolfgang Orlich. 9159 [2]

Albert Camus: L'Etranger. Herausgegeben von Brigitte Sahner. 9169 [2]

Anatole France: Crainquebille. / Les Juges intègres. Herausgegeben von Thomas Baldischwieler. 9162

Jean Giraudoux: La Guerre de Troie n'aura pas lieu. Herausgegeben von Norbert Weitz. 9163 [2]

Eugène Ionesco: La Cantatrice chauve. Herausgegeben von Diethard Lübke. 9164

Jean de La Fontaine: Fables. Mit Illustrationen von Gustave Doré. Herausgegeben von Wolfhard Keiser. 9182

Guy de Maupassant: Contes. Herausgegeben von Irmgard Rauthe-Welsch. 9153

Prosper Mérimée: Carmen. / Vision de Charles XI. Herausgegeben von Ortrud Ahlers. 9171 [2]

Jacques Prévert: Poèmes et Chansons. Herausgegeben von Monika Beutter und Hans-Dieter Schwarzmann. 9155

Jules Romains: Knock ou Le Triomphe de la Médecine. Herausgegeben von Thomas Baldischwieler. 9154 [2]

Antoine de Saint-Exupéry: Courrier Sud. Herausgegeben von Walburga Hülk. 9174 [2]

Jean-Paul Sartre: Morts sans sépulture. Herausgegeben von Marianne Meid. 9175 [2]

Jules Verne: L'Éternel Adam. Herausgegeben von Hajo Weber. 9186

Philipp Reclam jun. Stuttgart

Englische Lyrik
in zweisprachigen Anthologien

Altenglische Lyrik. Ausgew. und hrsg. von Rolf Breuer und Rainer Schöwerling. 7995 [3]

Amerikanische Lyrik. Vom 17. Jahrhundert bis zur Gegenwart. Ausgew. und hrsg. von Franz Link. Übers. von Annemarie und Franz Link. 9759 [6]

Coleridge, Samuel Taylor: Gedichte. Übers. und hrsg. von Edgar Mertner. 9484 [3]

Dickinson, Emily: Gedichte. Ausgew. und übers. von Gertrud Liepe. Nachw. von Klaus Lubbers. 7908 [3]

Englische Barockgedichte. Ausgew. und hrsg. von Hermann Fischer. 9315 [6]

Englische und amerikanische Balladen. Hrsg. von Gisela Hoffmann. 7842 [6]

Englische Sonette. Ausgew. und übers. von Gisbert Kranz. 8372 [3]

Gedichte der englischen Romantik. Ausgew., hrsg. und komm. von Raimund Borgmeier. 9967 [5]

Hopkins, Gerard Manley: Gedichte. Übers. von Ursula Clemen und Friedhelm Kemp. Hrsg. von Wolfgang Clemen. 9440 [3]

Mittelenglische Lyrik. Ausgew. und hrsg. von Werner Arens und Rainer Schöwerling. 9985 [3]

Moderne englische Lyrik. Ausgew., komm. und hrsg. von Willi Erzgräber und Ute Knoedgen. 9826 [7]

Die englische Literatur in Text und Darstellung

Gesamtherausgeber: Raimund Borgmeier

Band 1: Mittelalter. Hrsg. Heinz Bergner. 7764 [5] (erscheint 1985)
Band 2: 16. Jahrhundert. Hrsg. Horst Weinstock. 7765 [5]
Band 3: 17. Jahrhundert I. Hrsg. Rainer Lengeler. 7766 [5]
Band 4: 17. Jahrhundert II. Hrsg. Elmar Lehmann. 7767 [5]
Band 5: 18. Jahrhundert I. Hrsg. Dietrich Rolle. 7768 [5]
Band 6: 18. Jahrhundert II. Hrsg. Walter Pache. 7769 [5]
Band 7: 19. Jahrhundert I. Hrsg. Raimund Borgmeier. 7770 [5]
Band 8: 19. Jahrhundert II. Hrsg. Bernhard Reitz. 7771 [5]
Band 9: 20. Jahrhundert I. Hrsg. Hans Ulrich Seeber. 7772 [5]
Band 10: 20. Jahrhundert II. Hrsg. Raimund Borgmeier und Bernhard Reitz. 7773 [5] (erscheint 1985)

Einen hervorragenden Weg zur englischen Literatur eröffnet die Reclam-Reihe *Die englische Literatur in Text und Darstellung*. Zehn Bände führen vom Mittelalter bis in die Gegenwart. Die bisher erschienenen Bände sind überzeugend in der Auswahl der Texte und der Konzeption. Allgemeine Einleitungen und Einführungen zu den Werken wecken das Verständnis. Da alle Texte englisch und deutsch gebracht werden, kann man immer der originalen Gestalt begegnen. Alle Gattungen sind vertreten, und bibliographische Anhänge geben weiterführende Hinweise und Hilfen.

Bayerischer Rundfunk